101
Ways To Buy
Real Estate
WITHOUT
CASH

Wade Cook

Lighthouse Publishing Group, Inc.
Seattle, Washington

Lighthouse Publishing Group, Inc.

© 1998 by Wade B. Cook

"This publication is designed to provide accurate and authoritative information in regard to the subject matter covered. It is sold with the understanding that the publisher is not engaged in rendering legal, accounting, or other professional service. If legal or other expert as-sistance is required, the services of a competent professional person should be sought."
From a declaration of principles jointly adopted by a committee of the American Bar Association and a committee of the Publisher's Association.

This book was formerly a manual entitled "101 Ways To Buy Real Estate Without Cash." While some of the prices may not reflect current prices in some areas, the ideas are timeless and can still help the investor make a profit from implementing them.

Book Design by Judy Burkhalter
Cover Design by Mark Englebrecht

Library of Congress Cataloging-in-Publication Data
Cook, Wade
    101 ways to buy real estate without cash/Wade Cook.--2nd ed.
      p. cm.
    ISBN 0-910019-74-6 (alk. paper)
    1. Real estate investment--United States. 2. Real property--
United States--Purchasing. 3. Real estate business--United States.
I. Title. II. Title: One hundred one ways to buy real estate
without cash. III. Title: One hundred and one ways to buy real
estate without cash.
HD255.C638   1998
332.67'24--dc21   98-37362
                                                  CIP

Source Code: 101W98R2

Published by:
Lighthouse Publishing Group, Inc.
14675 Interurban Avenue South
Seattle, WA 98168-4664
1-800-706-8657 206-901-3100 (fax)
www.lighthousebooks.com

Printed in the United States of America
Second Edition
10 9 8 7 6 5 4 3 2

101
Ways To Buy Real Estate
WITHOUT CASH

Dedication

101 *Ways To Buy Real Estate Without Cash* is dedicated to all our real estate seminar students who have diligently studied and implemented these real estate strategies and found, to their delight and mine, that you really can get into real estate without cash!

Contents

Outline — ix

Thank You — xiii

Preface — xv

Section 1 — Why Real Estate? — 1

Section 2 — Seller Accepts Low Or No Money Down Deals — 13

Section 3 — The Seller Accepts Monthly Payments — 67

Section 4 — Getting Them The Money — 87

Section 5 — The Buyer Gets A Loan — 101

Section 6 — Partnerships — 151

Section 7 — Getting Them The Money Later — 187

Section 8 — Other Ways Of Getting Them The Money — 213

Section 9 — Ways To Find Good Deals — 271

Section 10 — Available Resources — 285

Outline

1   Total Owner Carryback 17
2   The Wraparound Mortgage 19
3   The Fixer-Upper: A Great Nothing Down Deal 21
4   Raise The Price, Lower The Terms 23
5   New First And/Or Second Mortgage And
    Seller Financing 25
6   New First And/Or Second Mortgage And Seller Fin-
    ancing, But With Buyer Taking Out New Mortgage 27
7   Rental Participation Technique 30
8   Give Them Three Choices 33
9   Trade-Offs 37
10 The Seller Who Must Move 39
11 Bad Tenants For Landlord Equal No Down
    Payment For You 42
12 Solving Problems Others Couldn't Solve 46
13 Assuming The Seller's Obligations 49
14 Down Payment In Monthly Payments 52
15 Lease With Option To Buy 54
16 Getting The Down Payment From
    Real Estate Agents 58
17 Seller Pays The Real Estate Commission Out
    Of His Equity, Not His Cash 60
18 Selling The Option Back To The Seller 62
19 The Desirability Of A Steady Monthly Income 71
20 Always Make The Seller Feel Secure 72

21   Get Them What They Want 74
22   Making A Wealthy Banker Out Of The Seller 75
23   My Special "Secret Weapon" 76
24   Blanket Mortgage To Make The Seller Feel Secure 77
25   Understanding The Seller's Needs 81
26   Refuse To Negotiate 82
27   High Tension Time Limit Technique 83
28   VA And FHA Loans 91
29   Conventional Loan: Second Mortgage Crank 95
30   Conventional Mortgage: First Mortgage Crank 98
31   Bank Loans For Down Payments 105
32   Home Equity Loans 107
33   Credit Cards 110
34   NOW Accounts 112
35   Buy Low, Refinance High 115
36   Combination: Small Down Payment Plus Graduated
       Monthly Payments 117
37   Establishing Commercial Credit 120
38   Local Finance Company Loans 123
39   Operating Line Of Credit 125
40   Commercial Loan: Short-Term Note 127
41   Letter Of Credit 129
42   Second Mortgage Crank 133
43   Created Paper 136
44   When The Seller Demands All Cash 139
45   Created Paper Two 142
46   Created Paper Three 145
47   VA And FHA Loans Two 148
48   Their Money, But Your Time And Talent 155
49   Using The Option To Buy To Split The Benefits 158
50   Using Credit Instead Of Cash 161

51   Using Your Partner's Equity Instead Of Your Cash 164
52   Using Your Partner's Personal Property Instead
     Of Cash 167
53   Using Your Partner's Work And Personal Property
     Instead Of Money 170
54   The "Fixer-Upper" Partner 172
55   Partners In Marriage And Real Estate 175
56   The Seller Can Be Your Partner 178
57   No Cash, Higher Income Partners 180
58   Limited Partners 182
59   Discounting Underlying Notes For Cash 183
60   Delayed Down Payment 191
61   Delayed Down Payment: Added Interest 192
62   Delayed Down Payment: Increase Price Of House 194
63   Delayed But Increased Down Payment 195
64   Mortgage Due In Six Months: All Cash 196
65   Mortgage Due In One Payment In Six Months:
     Offer Higher Price 198
66   Delayed Regular Mortgage: Raise Price Of House 199
67   Delayed Regular Mortgage: High Interest 201
68   Delayed Down Payment And Delayed Mortgage:
     Higher Price, Higher Interest 202
69   Moratorium On Interest Payments 204
70   One Great Deal Turned Into Three Terrific Deals! 206
71   Lump Sum In The Future 210
72   Using Furniture And Appliances For Down
     Payment 217
73   Selling Off Part Of The Property To Raise The
     Down Payment Money 219
74-76 Rental Deposits, Rent, & Real Estate Credits As
     Down Payments 221
77   Refurbishing Fees 225

78   Discounted Bonds 227
79   Option To Buy Discounted Notes 228
80   If Seller Sells To Someone Else 230
81   Discounted Mortgage Note As Down Payment 231
82   Creating Your Own Discounted Mortgage 234
83   Borrowing On The Certificate Of Deposit 237
84   Moving Private Mortgage From Senior Position
     To Junior Position 239
85   Making Mortgage Holder Your Partner 240
86   Getting Them Something They Want (Besides
     Cash) 243
87   Using A Lien On The Property To Get Them What
     They Want 245
88   Sweat Equity 247
89   Pay Full Price If Seller Accepts Well Secured Note
     For Equity 251
90   The Numbers Game 252
91   Buy And Sell At Same Price, And Make Money! 254
92   Houses, 20% Off! 255
93   Buying And Selling On Contract 257
94   Building A Real Estate Money Machine! 261
95   Cash Value Life Insurance: A Rich Source Of Money ... 263
96   The Option To Buy 267
97   Interest Rates And Monthly Payments You Can
     Live With 275
98   Interest Up Monthly Payments You Can Live With 276
99   An Exciting Idea 277
100 The Power Of Being In Control 281
101 Nothing Happens Until You Make An Offer 281

Thank You

101 *Ways To Buy Real Estate Without Cash* is a unique book, and so are the people who added extra insight into editing the original text. Without the following people, this book would not be the excellent idea source it is.

Catherine Coval, my Real Estate Seminar Director, and David Nelson, a real estate specialist, helped ensure that these ideas are still profitable today.

Many thanks goes to Lighthouse Publishing Group, Inc. and the Art Department who together produce excellent books. Special thanks goes to Cheryle Hamilton, Jerry Miller, Alison Curtis, Mark Engelbrecht, Vicki Van Hise, Angie Wilson, Connie Suehiro, Judy Burkhalter, Brent Magarrell, Cynthia Fliege, and Bethany McVannel.

Once again, I want to be sure to thank my wife, Laura, who inspires me every day to live above and beyond the average life.

Other Books By
Lighthouse Publishing Group, Inc.

Preface

Picture, if you will, a warm afternoon in early June. You have been traveling in your car up and down the streets of your home town looking for a vacant house, a house the lecturers spoke of in the seminars, the one the owners just have to get rid of to cover their own needs. You have been looking religiously for the past two weeks and you are a bit disgusted, wearisome, and just plain discouraged and tired of looking. You turn down Sunset Drive to make that final last effort before retiring to your favorite recliner, and . . . nothing.

All you see as you drive down the street is a poor attempt at a garage sale, and as you slowly pass you don't even see anyone there. The house built around the garage cannot be seen from the road due to the overgrowth of bushes and trees. "What an awful looking place," goes through your mind. "Who would ever want to live there? It would probably take thousands of dollars to ever make people pay attention to it. Why would anyone go to a garage sale there? Just a bunch of junk. The owners are probably making their last attempt before moving from that place. Who would want to even worry about an old wreck like that?" Suddenly your brain clicks . . . *you would*!!! This is what you've been searching for!

You do a 180° turn in the middle of the road and casually (at 75 mph) drive back to the garage sale, only to find your wildest dreams have come true. There in the midst of the shamble is a well structured, nicely roofed foundation house in need of ten hours of cosmetic fix-up, and it is FOR SALE.

Not only is it for sale, but the owners are willing to take a contract for their equity. $1,000 is needed for closing as long as you agree to close before their next payment is due in two weeks. They only want $45,000 for their house (worth closer to $72,000), but you will have to assume their payments of $400 per month at 6.5% interest on the underlying loan at closing. They just want out!

As your mind shifts into high gear and you trip over yourself getting into the car to find that earnest money agreement and your checkbook, you realize that all of the time and effort you have put in have paid off and you have reached a turning point in you life. You have struck it rich, and to think you almost didn't stop and look.

This is just the beginning. With this one success, you are now rejuvenated and ready to duplicate this memorable process. However, is this really the way you can be most effective in your search for financial independence while buying real estate? Inevitably, the "once in a lifetime deals" like the one on Sunset Drive will continue to turn up as you get more involved in good negotiations with the owners of all the properties you find.

It's great that you are learning that each encounter with the sellers and owners help you achieve your goals much faster. It leaves you in a more secure financial position. Think back to all of the houses you found before Sunset Drive where the owners wanted only cash down payments of $5,000, $10,000, and $20,000. These limitations imposed by the sellers' wants and needs will determine the amount of houses or investments you can get into, unless you learn to control each and every negotiation and down payment.

The reason you need this control is because *you* have limitations. You may be one of those who has a large bank roll or have a list of friends who fit that description. You may be one of the group of investors who has a certain amount of cash set aside ($2,000 to $10,000); once it is spent, it's over for you until you once again build your savings. You must learn to be in control. Not only will you feel better about your negotiations, but you will find or learn ways to cut the expense of large down payments, large burdensome assumptions with ridiculous bank qualifications, and limit your time to the points of true value to you.

Does a $10,000 cash down payment scare you away from what otherwise would be a great investment, when you know that you do not have or want to spend more than the $3,000 you have set aside for each property?

Do you walk away without facing the Negotiating Challenge? Are you losing time, money and patience with the programs you are seeking because you do not find these as plentiful and as necessary to build your income fast enough?

How can you use your cash in a non-spending fashion; that is, only as necessary, rather than as the first and only alternative you have as you begin negotiating?

Why is it so easy for owners to say they want cash down payments of up to 50% without even batting an eyelash? Why is the Cash Syndrome so important to the owner, or the real estate agent?

How can you spend less in purchasing so as to leave your cash free for closing expenses only?

Aren't there ways to buy houses and properties without spending money—at least not the cash you have in your own personal accounts?

If these are some of the questions you are encountering, perhaps you should explore ways to bring about the results you need *without* spending your cash. It is my attempt in this book to demonstrate and discuss in detail, a wide variety of purchasing methods that will give you *101 Ways To Buy Real Estate Without Cash.* These strategies work.

Section 1

Why
Real
Estate?

Why Real Estate?

Let's begin by taking an honest look at you and the reason you bought this book. You bought it to achieve three main goals:

First and foremost, your goal is to generate monthly income, also known as cash flow. This would, of course, allow you to improve your life-style. It would also allow you to say goodbye to the career you're in, which is taking you nowhere.

Second, you are seeking the tax advantages derived from real estate investments. These are perfectly legal benefits that range from low taxes to no taxes.

Not to be overlooked is reason number three: long term growth and retirement.

Real estate is the only form of investment that allows you to accomplish all three of these goals. I have studied over 200 types of investments and none offer the benefits of real estate.

A study done by the University of Michigan found that over 70% of all the millionaires in America have 50% or more of their assets in real estate.

In this book I have examples of average individuals who have a strong desire to succeed. I have detailed, step by step, the virtually unknown ways that any individual using hard work and enthusiasm can, as others have, change their life forever.

The key word here is enthusiasm. Through enthusiasm you acquire motivation. Motivation will see you through the toughest of times. This enthusiasm will be conveyed to your business acquaintances, friends and family.

I have found there is no real secret to success. Once you've been successful at one thing, you will be successful at another. Success has three principles. If you follow them, you virtually cannot fail.

First, you need to acquire the money for your venture. As soon as you do this, you can begin investing.

Second, you need to parlay your investments into a steady cash flow, or income, if you will.

Third is commitment. You will be amazed at the way your life will turn around as soon as you commit yourself to being successful. Every day you must write down your daily plan and commit to it. Remember: those who fail to plan, plan to fail.

Now that we have briefly discussed you and your goals, let's examine in greater detail real estate's three benefits: income, taxes, and growth equity.

There are five types of income. The first is rental income. This is received from being a landlord.

The second is tax income. The one aspect of real estate that sets it apart from most other forms of investment is that the purchase can be written off, legally. In fact, you may eventually find yourself foregoing a positive net monthly income in order to achieve a long range positive effect on your taxes.

The third is income from notes. These notes are acquired from taking our equity in the form of monthly payments. This is covered extensively further on in this book.

The fourth is derived from fees and commissions. We receive these when we invest money for others.

Finally, you receive income from your equity when you turn it into cash. In other words, when you sell a property and your buyer pays you cash for the equity in it.

The second benefit is in taxes. For years people have lectured and written volumes on the evils of taxation. Others spend time instructing individuals how to beat the tax system. Unfortunately, many of these books are typed on the machines at the local prison library.

It's so simple! The way to beat the IRS is to follow their own guidelines. In no other way can an individual ease his tax burden so substantially as by investing in real estate. And it is all legal. The most exciting by-product of this investing is your ability to literally zero out your taxes. For every $10,000 worth of income you receive, all you need is one good rental unit in the $80,000 to $100,000 range to seriously reduce your taxes.

The third benefit is growth equity. This is last only because income and tax relief demand immediate attention. However, because we devote so much time and effort to income and tax write offs, we end up with equity growth. The properties we acquire rise in value. Simply put, a property you purchased in 1978 for $75,000 could very well be valued at $125,000 today. Hence, growth equity. Increased income, selling, and borrowing power are all advantages of real estate investing.

The Money Machine Concept

Early in the 1970s, I developed a unique concept for acquiring real estate with little or no money down. I called it the Real Estate Money Machine. Using this concept I acquired a large amount of real estate and was soon on the way to financial independence. I then wrote the book **Real Estate Money Machine** and began conducting seminars on this unique approach to real estate investment. I am convinced, not only by my own success, but by the success of those who took part in my seminars, that the Money Machine concept is the most viable no money down method in the field today.

Let's look at this example: you want to buy a house at a price of $42,000. You are willing to pay $2,000 down because this is slightly less than 5%. Anytime you can buy a house for 5% down, you are ahead of the game.

The house has a $20,000 first mortgage and a $10,000 second mortgage. You assume these mortgages. After you have paid the seller $2,000 down on his $12,000 equity, he has $10,000 equity left in the house. You are willing to pay him 1% per month for his equity. This is $100 a month.

The place needs a little fixing up, so you spend $1,000 and do the necessary repairs. Now you sell the property to a new buyer.

After you have fixed the place up, it is worth $55,000 or $60,000. You sell the property to a new buyer for $53,000. You take $3,000 down payment from the new buyer.

Why $3,000? You bought the place for $2,000 down and you have just spent $1,000 fixing it up. You have $3,000 cash in this place. So you sell it for $53,000 with a $3,000 down payment.

This way you get your $3,000 back that you spent on the place. You can use this $3,000 to go out and work the concept all over again.

The new buyer has given you a $3,000 down payment on your $53,000 house. He now owes you $50,000. You sold the house on a wraparound mortgage, which means that the new buyer owes you the whole $50,000 on one mortgage. You do not let him assume the bottom loans, the $20,000 first mortgage and the $10,000 second mortgage. You keep making payments on the two bottom loans. The payments on these two mortgages total $400 a month. The new buyer is now making payments to you in the amount of $500 a month, which is 1% per month of the total mortgage of $50,000. You net $100 per month.

This is the money-machine concept in a nutshell.

Would it be better if you got more money down from the new buyer, say $4,000, $5,000, or even $6,000? Yes, this is what you should try to do. Always attempt to get more money back on the new buyer's down payment than you have actually invested in the house, your total investment being the down payment you made plus whatever money you have spent in repairs. If you have $2,000 invested in the property, try to get at least a $3,000 down payment from the new buyer when you sell the place. If you have $3,000 invested, try to get a down payment of at least $4,500 from the new buyer. A good rule is to add at least 50% to your total investment in the property, and ask this amount as a down payment from the new buyer.

The Real Secret In Getting Your Money Out Of A Property

The more money you put into a property, the harder it will be to get that money back out. This is because the higher the down payment you ask for, the tougher it will be to resell the house.

So the real secret of getting money back out of a property is this: don't put any money into the property in the first place!

This is a very good reason for paying little or no money down when you purchase property. Whenever you buy a house, always think of what you will have to do for the next buyer when you resell.

While interest rates in your area will vary, we could say in this example that I have never sold a house at 12% interest. If I take over a loan at 9 or 10%, I'll give the new buyer a wrap-around mortgage at 10$\frac{1}{2}$% interest.

Is this a good deal for the next buyer? Yes. Always remember this: nothing is going to sell unless you make a good deal for the next buyer.

Now let's think about this. We are talking about no money down deals. If you pay 5% or less on a down payment, it is classified as a little or nothing down deal. But if you can successfully resell that same house quickly, and receive a down payment from the new buyer at least as large as the down payment you gave the seller when you bought the house, you are getting all of your down payment back.

Does this make it a no money down deal for you? You bet it does! You've got your whole down payment back, plus a little more if you ask for a bigger down payment. You can use this same money and go out and do the whole thing over again.

This is the Real Estate Money Machine concept. You avoid banks, coming and going. You don't borrow money from the banks to buy the property, and you don't ask your new buyers to borrow money from the banks to pay you for your equity. You never make a dime on the interest the bank charges—you only make money on the interest you charge your buyers!

This is the essence of the Real Estate Money Machine. You buy your houses so that you make monthly payments to the seller. You sell your houses to get monthly payments coming in to you. If you do put a small down payment on a house, get that down payment back from the next buyer. You can quickly build up monthly payments as you continue to work this concept over and over.

Be A Banker, Not A Landlord!

The money machine does two great things for you. First, it effectively makes you a banker. You have the monthly payments coming in, including interest. Second, it keeps you from being a landlord. You avoid the thrill of management! You don't have all the problems that go with rentals.

You don't even have the problems of a property owner. You don't have to worry about maintenance or repairs. The new buyer is the property owner, and he is the one faced with all of those problems. You just sit back and watch your payments come in every month. This is a great way of building monthly cash flow.

Net Income Versus Gross Income

Many people talk about gross income and the gross value of their investments. One claims he has just gone out and bought 10 million dollars worth of real estate. He wants to impress you.

But who cares? Who cares about the gross amount?

What pays the bills every month? Gross value? Gross income? *No!* Net monthly income is what pays the bills every month and lets you retire. What you really need is a positive cash flow.

Everything we are talking about here is carefully designed to *build monthly income and net equity*. With the money machine, you build up your net equity by recycling your down payment over and over again, getting your down payment back when you resell the house, and buying another house with it.

Do A Lot Of Buying With A Little Money

The whole concept of buying property with little money down is the idea of keeping your money free to allow you maximum buying with minimum of money. If you have $10,000, don't spend it all on a down payment for one house. Instead, buy several properties with this money, giving much smaller down payments. Always make your down payments as small as possible, and eliminate them altogether when you can.

Then, whether you rent the properties, sell them on the money machine and get monthly payments, or just cash out the properties completely when you sell them, the law of leverage will always work with this concept. You will get better at it along with everything else you are doing in the field of real estate.

The law of leverage makes everything else happen.

Educating The Seller: Dispelling Wrong Ideas That Might Make Him Reject Your Offer

Every real estate investor should know that many sellers have formed their opinions and assumed their mindsets based upon fallacious thinking, unsupported myths, and second and third-hand stories, about how real estate works. Let's examine some of these fallacies:

1. My Uncle Henry told me that I could go ahead and sell investment property for all cash, and if I reinvested the proceeds within a certain number of months, I would not have to pay a dime in taxes on the profit.

This is definitely not true, but many people believe it. Your job is to educate the seller to the fact that this is a completely mistaken idea. If the seller makes a profit on the sale of his investment property, he will have to pay taxes on this profit! If he doesn't believe you, have him check with the IRS. They will convince him in short order!

2. I'm afraid to take back any paper on the sale of my property, paper like a mortgage or a deed of trust. If I'm holding a second mortgage and the first mortgage is not paid, the bank forecloses and I would lose everything!

This is *not true*! But again, this fear exists with many sellers. Have the seller focus on the true facts. You can take control of the property again, because you have rights as a second mortgage holder. If the seller does not believe you, refer him personally to the bank. They will set him straight fast!

3. My wife's third cousin knew a guy who sold his property, took back a mortgage on his equity in the property, and then never received a single payment from the shyster who bought it from him! They told him he couldn't do anything about it! He lost his property, and never got a dime out of it!

You don't know for sure whether this story happened at all. If it did really happen, then the man who sold the property and received no payments on it obviously never sought the advice of a lawyer. If he had retained even a mediocre lawyer, he would have gotten his property back.

4.   I've got to have all cash for my property. I want to buy another property, and unless I get all cash from you, I won't be able to purchase it.

Explain to the seller that over 70% of all house sales involve some sort of owner financing. So maybe the seller of this property will not need as much cash as he thinks in order to buy another house.

5.   If I take paper like a mortgage or trust deed when I sell property, I'm going to be stuck with that paper. There is no way I could possibly get cash for that paper without selling it at a tremendous loss.

Here you will have to educate the seller about how this paper can be effectively used for many profitable purposes. It can be used as collateral in borrowing money, it can be used as a down payment on another property, or the owner of the paper can sell the income from the paper for lump sum cash.

I have used this opening section to briefly discuss you, your future, and the advantages of investing in real estate. In the pages that follow, you will find proven ways to achieve your financial independence, often without having to use one cent of your own money. Remember, genuine enthusiasm and diligent effort will always get the job done.

Section 2

Seller Accepts Low Or No Money Down Deals

Seller Accepts Low Or No Money Down Deals

When you plan to make an offer on a property, you naturally want to get the best deal for your money, but so does the seller. In this section, you will learn some secrets of negotiation so you will be ahead in the long run and have a satisfied seller. Your seller may have different plans than you do, but as you negotiate and show that it's in his best interest to accept a "no" or "low-money" down deal, he will wrap his mind around your offer as he understands the benefits of doing so. Put the seller in the driver's seat and let them make their own decisions.

Who do you think is the best person to make decisions for you when you're getting ready to buy a house? You are! And who do you think has a lot of great ideas about the price, terms and curb appeal of a house? You do! So, who do you want to have making the choices and decisions about the purchase of a house? Well, naturally, you do. And so does the seller. Keep this in mind as you prepare your offer; don't give them just one of-fer—give them three! They like to be in control of the sale just as much as you do, so prepare your three best offers, giving and taking, and negotiate from there. This section will give you sev-eral scenarios of how I did just that.

Total Owner
Carryback

1

Suppose you find a property you would like to acquire with a fair market value (FMV) of $50,000. It has an existing assumable mortgage of $30,000 at 8% interest per year, with payments of $245 per month. The seller's equity in the house is $20,000.

You offer the seller the basic no money down deal. You tell him, "I like your house very much and I really want to buy it. It's worth $50,000, and I'm willing to give you that much for it. But I can't give you that much all at once. I can do this, though. I can go ahead and assume your mortgage for $30,000 with the bank. I'll start making these payments to the bank immediately. I know that you have $20,000 worth of equity in the house over and above your mortgage. I can pay you this $20,000 for your equity and buy your house if you will let me pay it off in monthly payments. I'll give you a $20,000 second mortgage on the house at 11% interest per year. I will be making monthly payments of $200 to you."

At first, the seller is shocked by your offer. He says, "I want my $20,000 *now!* I can't afford to wait around and let that $20,000 dribble in at a rate of $200 a month!"

You reply, "There are three reasons why you might rather have this paid off in monthly payments as opposed to getting the $20,000 all at once. The first reason is that you could save yourself a lot of money on taxes."

His eyes light up with real interest at the mention of the word taxes. "How would it save me money on taxes?"

You explain, "If I pay you $20,000 cash right now, you have to declare the whole thing on your income taxes for this year. Do you know how much tax you would have to pay on that? It would probably jump you into a higher tax bracket, too, so you would be paying a higher percentage on your regular income for the year, as well as the $20,000 extra for the sale of your house."

"You're right," he says. "There really would be a big advantage as far as taxes are concerned. What are the other two reasons you mentioned?"

You continue, "This will give you a regular steady monthly income. You can use this steady monthly income to help you with your retirement, or use it to buy something you want—a car, or furniture, or anything else you would like. You could use these monthly payments to make monthly payments on something else you would like to buy."

"That's true," he admits. "It would be nice to have a steady monthly income."

"And the third reason is this: this money will not pay off quickly. At $200 per month, I will be making these payments to you for twenty years or more. You will end up with far more money in the long run than if I gave you $20,000 cash right now. You will end up with something more like $60,000 than $20,000."

He makes his decision. "All right, you've got yourself a deal."

Congratulations! You've just bought a house with no money down!

This is really the ultimate in no down payment financing. It is called the "paper-out." The name comes from the simple reason that the seller wants to "get out" of his property so desperately that he is willing to take a note, or "paper" from you, with no down payment in the form of cash.

Why would any seller do this? You can rest assured that he has a very pressing reason for selling the property. He is called a "Don't-Wanter." This is the term used to describe a highly motivated seller. He has some kind of ownership problem. When you come to him with your offer, you will replace his ownership problem with a steady positive cash flow from your paper.

You can sometimes even do better than this, and set up the deal so that you will not be making any monthly payments at all for awhile. The secret is all in negotiation.

The Wraparound Mortgage

2

You answer an ad in the newspaper and find a single family dwelling for sale by owner. It has a fair market value of $60,000 with an existing assumable first mortgage of $30,000 at 8% interest, with payments of $245 per month. The seller's equity is $20,000.

You meet with the owner and present your program. You offer to pay the full $50,000. You agree to assume the first mortgage and begin making payments right away. Then you offer a second mortgage to the seller for the $20,000 equity in the house, and offer to pay $200 a month at 10% interest.

This would give you total monthly payments of $445: the $200 per month to the seller and $245 per month to the bank on the first mortgage.

At this point, the seller might be a bit dubious, and say, "What if something happens and you start missing payments on the first mortgage to the bank? Then the bank might foreclose and I would lose my house."

You make him another offer. "As long as you are still making payments in your first mortgage with the bank, you feel secure, right? You know the bank is not going to foreclose on you."

The seller nods. "As long as I'm the one who is making the payments, I know the payments are always going to be made and I know I'm not going to lose the house to the bank."

"Then let's do this," you say. "You continue to make your regular payments to the bank on the first mortgage, and I will make all my monthly payments directly to you. I'll give you what they call a wraparound mortgage."

"A wraparound mortgage? What is that?"

"It works like this," you say. "I'm buying your house at a price of $50,000. I'll give you a mortgage on the whole $50,000, and make you payments of $445 per month, at a 10% rate of interest. This way, I will be paying the same amount of money that I would have paid to you and to the bank together, only this way, I will pay the whole $445 to you. Then you can take $245 out of that every month and pay the bank your own monthly payments on your first mortgage. As long as you are making your payments to the bank, you'll never have to worry about the bank foreclosing on you."

The seller understands what you're talking about now. To him, that sounds like a much better arrangement. You tell the seller, "On the surface, you appear to be getting the same deal as far as the money is concerned. But in reality you are getting a much better deal than that."

"Really?" asks the seller, "How much better?"

You sit down at the table with him and start putting figures down on a piece of paper. "Let's look at the actual affect here. I'm paying you $5,000 per year in interest. That is 10% of $50,000 per year. You are netting the difference of $2,600 per year. Your equity is $20,000, so you are actually netting 13% per year on this transaction. $2,600 is 13% of $20,000, and that is the equity you are receiving the interest on."

He studies the figures on the paper. "That's right," he says, "and that's a higher interest rate than 10%. What's happening here?"

"Just this. I'm paying you 10% interest per year on the entire $50,000 value of your house. But you don't actually own $50,000 worth of this house! You actually own only $20,000 worth of equity in this house. The bank owns the other $30,000.

That means I am paying you 10% interest on the $30,000 worth of your house still owned by the bank."

You go on. "You are paying off your first mortgage with the bank at a much faster rate than my wraparound mortgage of $50,000 to you. This means that your equity, which is starting out at $20,000 right now, is actually going to be growing in value each year. When your first mortgage is paid off in 15 years or so, my wraparound mortgage to you will still have an unpaid balance of about $35,000!"

The seller studies the figures on the paper in front of him. He finally says, "This isn't a good deal. This is a great deal!"

This is really a win/win transaction for you *and* the seller.

The Fixer-Upper: A Great Nothing Down Deal   3

The very fact that a house is a fixer-upper means it is a natural to become a nothing down deal. The owner really knows what condition the house is in, and he wants to sell it "as is." He knows someone is going to have to spend the money required for repairs. He also knows that he does not want to have to be the one spending that money. Or maybe he doesn't have the money to make the necessary repairs.

So you come along and present your offer. "Mr. Jones, I know that you want $2,000 down for your property, but your home really does need some fixing up, and I just don't have enough money to make the down payment and still fix the house up the way it should be. I'll need to keep all the money I have in order to fix up the house after I buy it."

"If you let me use my $2,000 to fix this place up instead of on a down payment, it's going to be worth a lot more than it is right now. This will raise the actual value of the property, and there will be more equity in it above the mortgage you have on it right now."

You continue, "This will make your position much more secure. After I spend my money to fix the place up and the equity is increased, I will own that extra equity. This means that if I ever stop making payments to you, you can go ahead and foreclose on the house, and I will lose all my equity as well as the house. I would have more to lose if I lost the house, and you would have more to gain if you got the house back."

Think about this. Would you rather spend your money on someone else's equity, or fix up the property and gain equity of your own? When you use your money to fix up that property, you are gaining equity; usually more equity, dollar for dollar, than the money you are actually spending on it.

I do not like spending my cash for someone else's equity. I will trade in my cash to buy potential, but not the other person's equity. When someone says he has equity in his property, that is his problem. I'm not going to give him cash for his equity. I would rather keep my cash and go out and buy something I really want, like a TV, car or computer.

Cash for equity is not a fair trade. You trade something that is very liquid for something that is not. If you put cash into a property, you had better be figuring out a way to get that cash back when you want it.

Never put yourself in a position where you are short of cash.

Raise The Price, Lower The Terms

4

Here is a technique which is very effective in persuading the seller to accept your no down payment offer.

Suppose you are out scouting around and discover a nice eight-unit apartment building for sale by owner. You walk into the manager's office and say, "Hello, Mr. Dalton. I am seriously considering buying your apartment building here. What price are you asking for it?"

"The selling price is $100,000."

"That sounds like a fair price," you say. "Do you have an existing mortgage on it?"

"No," he replies. "I own this building outright."

"Are you willing to take monthly payments on it?" you ask.

He thinks about it. "Yes," he replies slowly, "I would be willing to take monthly payments, if you would be willing to give me a large enough down payment on it, and if you pay me a high enough rate of interest."

"How high a down payment are you talking about?" you ask, "and how high an interest rate?"

Mr. Dalton considers. "I would like at least a 10% cash down payment. That would be $10,000 cash. I would be willing to carry the balance on the mortgage at an interest rate of 12% per annum." From what you've learned, you don't have to consider his proposal for long. There is no way you can raise $10,000 cash for a down payment. And it is definitely against your principles to pay an interest rate of 12% or higher. You reply, "That would be a fair deal. The only trouble is I just could not raise $10,000 cash right now. But how about this? I'm willing to give you $105,000 for your apartment building. In return for this, I would like you to forget the cash down payment, and give me a mortgage on the whole of $105,000 at a rate of 10% interest per year. This way you will be getting 2% less interest, but 5% more in capital gains."

He considers your offer. Then he says, "That's a decent offer. But I would still like something as a down payment."

You present another offer to him. "I will be making regular monthly payments to you at 1% per month on the principle of $105,000. That would be $1,050 a month. A good portion of each of those payments will be interest. Let me give you your $10,000 down payment. I'll pay you an extra $1,000 at the end of every year for ten years. This will give you your $10,000. And I would like each $1,000 payment deducted from the principle, without any interest deducted from it. Would that be fair enough?"

He looks very interested. "That's coming closer to what I could live with. I would still like the money sooner than that, though. Would you be willing to make those extra $1,000 payments every six months instead of every year?"

You say, "I'm willing to do that."

He smiles and shakes your hand. "You've just bought yourself an apartment building."

You can afford to give him that extra $5,000 in the long run to avoid paying the $10,000 cash down payment right now. Even if the apartment building is worth $5,000 less than what you are paying in the long run, it will appreciate at the rate of 10% per year. This means that the first year, your $100,000 apartment building will be worth $110,000. Long before your loan is paid off on this property, it will be worth considerably more than your $105,000 purchase price.

This is the principle: you raise the price you are willing to pay for the property in exchange for lower terms; the lower interest rate and the complete elimination of the cash down payment. The seller is easily able to see that he is getting a trade-off.

He is giving you a benefit by eliminating the cash down payment and lowering the interest rate. He knows that in return he is receiving a higher price for his property. This is just a simple trade of benefits.

Use it! It works!

New First And/Or Second Mortgage And Seller Financing **5**

You find an ad in the newspaper offering a home for sale by owner. The price of the house is $50,000. You phone the owner and make an appointment to see the house.

Upon arrival you see that the house is located in a respectable neighborhood. The house itself is in good condition and well worth the asking price of $50,000.

You introduce yourself to the owner. "Your ad said you're asking $50,000 for the house. Do you have an assumable mortgage on it?"

"Yes. The mortgage stands at about $20,000. The interest rate is $8^{1}/_{2}\%$."

This means he has $30,000 worth of equity in his home. You ask if he would be willing to let you pay monthly payments on the equity.

The owner looks a little shocked. "On the whole $30,000? No, I'm afraid we couldn't do that. Jane and I have been planning to go to Hawaii when we sell the house, and we're going to need the cash."

You can see no way of arranging a trip to Hawaii on monthly payments. So you try a different idea. "All right, then. What is the least amount of cash down payment you could get by on?"

He replies, "I think we've really got to have something like $8,000 cash."

"And you'd be willing to take the balance on monthly payments?"

"Yes," he says, "I think we could get by on that."

"Then let's do this," you say. "You have plenty of equity on your house above your $20,000 first mortgage. You can easily go back to your bank and get a second mortgage on that equity. You could take out a second mortgage and borrow the $8,000 cash you want right now."

"*Borrow* the money?" He is amazed. "I don't want to *borrow* more money on my own house. I've spent years paying off this much. I want to sell the house and get the cash. If I borrowed the money, I would just have to turn around and start paying it back a month at a time. I really don't want to do that."

"You won't have to pay it back," you reply. "You won't have to ever pay it back. I am the one who is going to be paying that money back."

He looks at you. "What? Why would you pay it back and how can I be sure you would?"

"Because I will be buying your house from you. I would take over your first mortgage and begin making monthly payments on it. When I buy your house, I would take over your second mortgage along with the first one, and make those monthly payments also. You'll not only have your $8,000 down payment, but you'll be clear out of the picture. I'll be making all the payments to the bank and you'll be in Hawaii with your $8,000, along with the regular monthly payments I'll be making to you for the equity in your house."

Mr. Peterson looks undecided. "That does sound as though it might work. However, . . . "

"Let's call your bank right now," you say. "Ask them if they would lend you $8,000 on your $30,000 equity in your house." He agrees to call the bank. After a brief conversation with his loan officer, he hangs up and turns to you. "They'll do it!" he exclaims.

"They'll lend us more than $8,000, if we want it. And as long as we're going to be doing it this way, I'll borrow $10,000 instead of $8,000."

You smile. "Great! We'll just make that second mortgage for $10,000 then, and that will be my down payment to you. Shall we sit down and write up the agreement?"

"Let's write it up!" says Mr. Peterson.

New First And/Or Second Mortgage And Seller Financing, But With *Buyer* Taking Out New Mortgage

6

You are fresh from your success in buying the Peterson home and the Petersons have sent you a nice "Aloha" card from Hawaii. So when you find this lovely home out in the suburbs at a price of $60,000, you are all set to do the same thing again that succeeded so well with the Petersons.

You walk up to the house and knock on the door. The door opens and you find yourself face to face with a large burly man with tattoos on his forearms. You sense right away that this man is not going to be exactly like Mr. Peterson.

Once introductions are completed you present your program.

"Do you have a mortgage on your house?" you ask.

"Yeah, $22,000."

"And you're asking $60,000 for the house?" you ask.

"Yeah."

"Then that gives you an equity of $38,000."

"I guess so," he says.

You have already learned that property owners sometimes do not know how much equity they have in their houses, or even what their monthly payments are.

You continue, "Well, Mr. McGraw, I would really like to buy your house, and I can manage it if you will let me assume your mortgage with the bank and then just make monthly pay-ments on the balance of your equity."

Mr. McGraw scowls at you. "No way," he says flatly.

You look at the seller. When he says "No way," you can bet your life there is *no way!*

So you try the technique that worked so effectively with Mr. Peterson. You say, "How about if I give you a decent down payment, and then give you monthly payments for the rest of your equity, legally secured by a second mortgage to you on your equity in the house?"

His scowl relaxes, "How much of a down payment are you talking about?"

You deliberately start out low. "How about $5,000?"

The seller shakes his head. "Not enough. Make it $10,000."

You think about asking him if he would be willing to split the difference and make it $7,500, but when you take a good look at that grim-jawed determination stamped on Mr. McGraw's face, you think better of it. He is in no mood to compromise on that $10,000. "That's agreeable," you say. "A $10,000 down payment would be fine. I don't actually have that much cash for a down payment, but I can tell you how we can arrange it so we can get the down payment for you."

He looks suspicious. "How's that?" he demands.

"This is what we can do. You have $38,000 equity in your house. You can easily arrange a second mortgage on that equity through your own bank, and borrow the $10,000 for your down payment. Then I take over both your first mortgage and your second mortgage and make the payments on them, and you keep that $10,000 for your down payment. I'll give you a third mortgage on the rest of your equity, and start making payments to you every month."

Mr. McGraw clamps his jaw shut. "No way," he grits through his teeth. "I'm not taking out any loan on my own house for your down payment to me."

You nod quickly and say as inoffensively as possible, "I can see how you feel about that. That was just a suggestion, I would never ask you to do anything like that if you don't really want to do it. So I'll get you your $10,000 down payment in a different way."

"What way?" he queries.

"I'll go ahead and buy your house and assume your first mortgage. You don't have to take out any second mortgage at all. I'll take out that second mortgage myself, right after we close the deal and the house is in my name. I'll borrow that $10,000 on a second mortgage in my name, and give you that $10,000 for your down payment."

"Hmmm," growls the seller. "How do I know you're going to pay that $10,000 to me after the close? You'd already have my house then, and I wouldn't have any down payment to show for it. Do you think I would take your *word* that you'd pay me that $10,000 after you had the house in your name? No way."

"No," you reassure him. "I wouldn't ask you to rely on just my word alone. I would sign a completely binding legal agreement to take out that second mortgage and pay you off in 90 days. The agreement can be secured by a quit claim deed, which can be held by a title company."

The suspicious scowl slowly disappears from Mr. McGraw's face. He puzzles over it a bit longer, trying to see if there is any way he could possibly be cheated on this deal. He finally nods slowly. "You've got yourself a deal," he says.

On techniques #5 and #6, the seller had the benefit of receiving a large amount of cash as a down payment, and you purchase the house with no cash down. But here is a word of caution: since the interest rate on the new mortgage with the bank will probably be fairly high, it is very important for you to negotiate a below market interest rate on any mortgage the seller takes back on his equity in the property. Always do this, and your use of these two similar techniques will enable you to buy houses successfully with no money down, and still keep your monthly payments at levels low enough to enable you to resell the property at a higher monthly payment, thus making a profit but still passing along a monthly payment that the new buyer can live with.

7   Rental Participation Technique

You have been looking for an apartment building to purchase. Every day you have been scanning the newspaper looking for ads offering rental units for sale.

You find a ten-unit apartment building in a nice section of town, close to the university, the shopping center and local schools. You can see you should not have any trouble keeping these units rented. You contact the owner, introduce yourself and tell him you might be interested in the apartment building that is advertised for sale.

You inquire, "What price are you asking for the property, Mr. Simons?"

"$125,000. $60,000 of that is my own equity. I'd like a $10,000 down payment in cash. Could you handle that?"

"I'd have to see the place first," you reply. "If I have the time, I might drop by this morning and have a look at it. Will you be there?

You don't want to appear too eager about buying the property. If you tell him, "I'll be there to see the place just as soon as I can. I'll be there in thirty minutes," Mr. Simons would probably consider you a highly motivated buyer and be expecting a high down payment, high interest rate, and high monthly payments. This is the last thing you want him to be thinking about when you walk in the door and face him.

Mr. Simons tells you he will be in all morning.

At this point, he is unsure of you. He only *hopes* you will come by to see the place. And, he *hopes* you will like it enough that you will be willing to purchase it. This way, he will be in the mood to give and take in a negotiation with you.

You drive out to the apartment building, walk up to the manager's office, and ring the doorbell. A small, pleasant-faced man comes to the door. "Hello," he says. "I'm Mr. Simons. Are you Jim Taylor?"

"That's right," you say. "I'd like to take a good look at your apartment building."

"Fine," says Mr. Simons. "I'll show you one of the rental units. They're all about the same."

You go with him and take a really good look at the rental unit he shows you. It seems to be in good condition. It is also obviously occupied. Clothes are hanging in the closet, and personal belongings are on the tables and shelves.

This is a good sign. You turn to the seller and say, "Are all these rental units occupied at the present time?"

"Yes," he says. "We're fairly close to the university here, and many of our renters are university students. We don't have any trouble keeping these units occupied."

Then you ask him this. "How long has it been since you raised the rent here?"

He rubs his chin, thinking. "About a year and a half."

"Are you able to raise the rent a little regularly, to keep up with inflation?"

"Oh yes," he says. "All the landlords in this area have been able to raise the rents on a fairly regular basis."

This is what you have been leading up to very carefully. Now you make him your offer. "You have a good apartment building here, Mr. Simons, and I'd like to buy it from you. Your price is right and I'm willing to pay it. Is your mortgage at the bank assumable?"

"Yes, it is," he says. "You won't have any difficulty assuming the loan."

"Will you take monthly payments for your equity?"

He looks at you directly. "If the conditions are right, I might consider it. I would need the $10,000 cash down payment, and a 13% interest on the second mortgage I would carry back from you."

This is what you were expecting him to offer. You reply to this, "That seems like a reasonable offer. But how about this? You say the rents are raised regularly in this area, and it looks as though they're about due for another raise right now. Is that right?"

He nods. "That's right. I think all the landlords will be raising the rent again soon."

"Then let's do this," you say, "for the next five years, I will give you 10% of all the increases in rents on this property. In exchange, I would like to buy your apartment building with no down payment, and with an interest rate of 10%. That way, you would be staying in for a percentage of the increased revenue generated by this apartment building. You really do believe that the rents are going to increase regularly, don't you?"

The seller looks a little surprised, but he is thinking over your offer. "Yes," he replies. "I don't know quite what to think of your offer, though. Ten percent seems a little low. Could you make that 11%? And how about seven years on the rental increases?"

You nod. "I can handle 11% for seven years."

Mr. Simons thinks a little bit longer. Then he says, "Your offer does seem a bit unusual, however, I can see its merits. I'm willing to sell to you on these terms."

Give Them Three Choices

8

This technique is quite enjoyable and highly effective in practice. People enjoy choices. They enjoy being in the driver's seat and having some control of the situation. They have to think about what they are doing, and they have to try to understand what is really going on.

If you walk into a seller's house and make one offer, the husband and wife look at that one offer, try to understand it, but maybe they don't have anything else to compare it with. The three of you sit down and try to work out an earnest money agreement, scratching all over it, crossing out things, putting in other things, and everyone putting initials in the proper places. This can be very confusing to them, and they feel at a loss. They are not sure they understand what is happening.

The solution to this is simple, effective, and can even be fun. Just walk in and give that husband and wife *three choices*, right in the beginning. This will give them a real chance to compare these three choices and the various merits of each one. As they compare the three choices, they will see for themselves just what the seller and the buyer are doing when they are "trading off" one thing for another.

Here is an actual example from my own experience: I found a nice duplex for sale at a price of $60,000. The people had a $45,000 FHA loan on it, and this loan was assumable. They had $15,000 equity in the property, and that's just what they wanted, $15,000 in cash.

I walked in and made them three offers.

A. I would buy the house at their asking price of $60,000. I would assume the $45,000 FHA loan on it, and I would make the seller's payments on their $15,000 equity. I would pay them $100 a month for the first two years, and then $150 a month beginning the third year and throughout the balance of the loan, until the entire loan was paid off. I would not give a down payment on this offer. Also, both the sellers and I would have our fair share of the closing costs. This would be a great selling price for the sellers. It would be a great deal for me as far as not having to make any down payment.

B. If I made them a lower offer on the purchase price, what would I have to offer the sellers? I was going to have to give them some cash down. So I offered them $3,000 cash as a down payment, and I offered them $58,000 purchase price for the duplex. This left them $10,000 equity in the property, and I gave them the same terms on their equity. I would pay them $100 a month for the first two years and $150 thereafter, until the balance of the loan was completely paid off.

C. My third offer was totally unique. I offered them a price of $55,000 with $2,000 cash down, and $8,000 at the end of three years. I would not make any payments on this $8,000 until the end of three years, and then I would give them the full $8,000 at the end of three years, with no interest added to the $8,000. And I would assume their $45,000 FHA loan and make their regular monthly payments on that.

Would I be buying equity with offer C? Certainly, I would. The duplex was really worth $60,000. I was offering $2,000 cash down payment, and I would be getting $5,000 worth of equity for this $2,000 since I was buying a $60,000 duplex at a $55,000 price. This way, I would have a head start to enable me to refinance the duplex, or do something with it down the road.

How about offer B? That was a big mistake on my part, by the way. I should not have offered them $58,000 on the purchase price there. $57,000 or even $56,000 would have been more appropriate.

The point is this: I gave them three choices. Who was in the driver's seat now? They were.

So, guess what they finally wanted to do? What was their final choice? They wanted to mix and match the best parts of each choice I gave them!

They said, "We'll take $60,000, with $3,000 in cash down right now, and the balance of $12,000 at the end of three years."

That is what will come back to you sometimes, the best of all three worlds. This happens 20 to 40% of the time.

However, most people are pretty straightforward. They see what you are doing here: the higher the price, the lower the down payment. The lower the total buying price, the more you are willing to give them in terms and cash.

Here is another example from my own experience: I found a probate case. This was a 1 1/2 bedroom house and it was ugly. I thought it looked like it might be worth $20,000, if it were fixed up.

This is different, because a judge was putting it up for sale. This was not quite like walking into someone's home and making him an offer. Making an offer to a judge is a completely different case.

Nevertheless, I made that judge three separate offers. I gave him three choices. He was a judge; I thought I would give him three offers to judge.

A. First, I offered to pay $8,000 for the purchase price, no cash down, and $80 a month in monthly payments.

B. My next offer was still $8,000 for the purchase price, but this time I would pay $2,000 down in cash, and $50 a month in payments until the rest of it was paid off.

C. I offered $8,000 for the purchase price, with no cash down and no payments. But I would pay the full $8,000 in cash at the end of three years.

I gave that judge three separate earnest money agreements, along with three different numbered checks, each one for $500 in earnest money.

The judge deliberated over these three choices, and he did make a judgement on them. He accepted my offer of $8,000, with no cash down and $80 a month in monthly payments. I had to pay only $250 in closing costs, and the house was mine.

This was a really hot deal for me! I knew the property was worth about $19,000 or $20,000. We fixed it up and sold it at a price of $29,000!

The point is this: put people in the driver's seat. Give them choices. Let them make their own decisions. When you give them choices, they start getting the message. If they want a down payment from you in cash, they're going to have to lower the selling price of their house. If they are willing to forego the down payment, they can get more money for their house in the long run. Just present them with the choices, and then let them use their own judgement and make the final decision.

Trade-Offs 9

When you are in the act of negotiating, the whole concept is trade-offs. Whenever somebody starts asking me for more cash as a down payment, I have a couple of choices. I can say this, "I'll give you a little bit more down if you are willing to lower the purchase price. I'll pay you $4,000 cash down instead of $3,000, but then I would like to pay you 9% interest on the balance, instead of 10%."

At this point, if the sellers really want or need that extra $1,000 in cash, then they are willing to lower the selling price of their house. Otherwise, they back off and leave the cash down payment at $3,000 and take the full selling price of their house.

Suppose a person says, "I need a $5,000 cash down payment instead of $3,000 down."

Then I say, "Okay, I'll give you the $5,000 cash down, if you are willing to meet me halfway. If I give you that $5,000 cash down payment, I would like to lower the selling price of the house by $2,000, and then drop my monthly payments to you from $350 a month to $325 a month."

I constantly do this. This trade-off concept can make a lot of money for you. The idea is this: I'll scratch your back if you'll scratch mine.

If you want to buy a house with a low cash down payment, or no down payment at all, you can use this trade-off concept effectively. Offer the seller a little more money on the purchase price of his house in return for a low cash down payment or no down payment at all. However, make certain that the monthly payments are ones you can live with. You can afford to give a higher purchase price because the house will be appreciating in value through inflation, and you can always resell the house later at a profit.

Let's take an example. Suppose you find a $60,000 house for sale by owner. You are in the house talking to the owner and he says, "I've got to have a $3,000 cash down payment on this, or it's no deal."

You think about that $3,000 cash. You really don't want to pay that much of a down payment. However, the house looks as though it is worth at least $60,000, and maybe even $65,000. Remember, you operate by this general rule: for every dollar you pay in cash, you want to get at least $2 worth of equity in the property you are buying.

So you say this to the seller of the house, "Well, what I would really like to do here is just assume your mortgage and start making you monthly payments on your equity. If you've really got to have the $3,000 cash down payment, I'll go ahead and give it to you, but if I give you that $3,000 cash, then I'd like to buy your house at a purchase price of $54,000. If you're willing to settle for a price of $54,000, I'm willing to give you your $3,000 in cash."

This surprises him for a moment, and he thinks about it.

"Or if you like," you continue, "I'll give you $58,000 for your house, with $1,500 down in cash. If you don't need all that cash right now, you'll make a lot more money on your house in the long run. I'll buy it with no down payment, and go ahead and pay you the full $60,000. When you add all the interest I'll be paying you in monthly payments, for every dollar's worth of equity I'm buying in your house, I'll eventually be giving you $3 in cash."

The seller thinks it over. Usually he forgets the down payment.

When you explain to the seller what you are doing, and your logical reasons for doing it, he feels better toward you. He understands why you are making the offers you are making, and feels more comfortable with the situation. He sees that you are willing to trade one thing for another, and realizes that it's in his own power to trade something he wants for something else he wants. He has to decide which he wants most, a large down payment in cash right now, or a larger selling price for his house and more equity which will be bringing in three times the amount of equity in dollars when paid to him in monthly payments over the years.

When he understands this, he has a clear choice to make, and he will be able to understand what he is doing when he makes the choice.

As for you, your first choice should be to buy that house with no down payment at all. However, if the seller makes one of the other choices, you can still live with the situation. Just remember to always offer $1,000 in cash as a down payment in return for $2,000 equity in the house. You lower the purchase price of the house $2,000. This gives you a comfortable margin to work with if you resell the house immediately. If the house is really worth $60,000 and you pay $58,000 for it, then you can turn around and resell it at a price of $60,000, getting your $1,000 cash down payment returned to you in the form of a down payment by the new buyer.

The Seller Who Must Move 10

Every day you are scanning the newspaper in the "House for Sale" ads. One morning you find one which reads: "Must sell—owner transferred."

You circle that one in a hurry and call the number in the ad. A woman answers the phone. You introduce yourself and request an appointment to see the property as soon as possible. She invites you over for 10:00AM.

Again, you never want to appear too eager in dealing with the seller. Always keep that "laid back" attitude.

You drive out to the house and arrive at about 10:30. The house looks nice, and the neighborhood is respectable. You walk up to the door and ring the doorbell.

A young woman answers the door. "Good morning, you must be the who called about the house."

"Yes," you say, "my name is Jim Taylor."

"My name is Sheila Rasmussen. My husband, Bob, isn't here. His company promoted him and he's in San Diego."

"How long has he been gone?"

"Oh, it seems like forever!" she exclaims. "But, actually, it's only been about a month. The kids and I miss him terribly."

"I'll bet he misses you too," you reply. You are just chatting with her now, getting her personal story and her feelings about her situation. "I guess you can't really be with him, until you sell the house?"

She nods. "Yes, we've got to sell the house before the kids and I can join him."

"I'd like to buy your house," you say, "if the price and terms are right. It looks very nice."

"Oh, yes," she replies, "it's been a very nice home for us. We think it's worth about $63,000, but we're willing to sell it for $60,000, so we don't have to wait a long time before it sells."

"How much money do you owe the bank on your mortgage?" you ask.

"$34,000," she says. "So we need to ask $26,000 for our equity in the house."

"That sounds like a fair price," you say. "Is your loan at the bank an assumable loan?"

"Yes, it is. Bob talked with them about it before he left for San Diego. If you buy the house, you can just take over the monthly payments."

"All right," you say. "I do like your house, and I do want to buy it from you. Will you let me pay you monthly payments on your equity in the house?"

"Oh," she looks a little disappointed. "Bob and I never discussed that. I just don't know what to say."

"Well, I'll just go ahead and make you an offer, and you can discuss it with Bob later. I'll pay you your full asking price of $60,000, with no down payment. I'll give you back a second mortgage on your $26,000 equity in the house, at 10% interest per year. I'll give you monthly payments on that loan at a rate of 1% per month on the total equity in your house. That means I will be paying you $260 every month, until I have paid off the whole $26,000. And when you talk with Bob about this, be sure and point out that by the time this $26,000 loan is paid off, you will really have received about three times that much, about $78,000."

Her eyes light up. "Oh, really? You mean we will actually get about $78,000 in payments on a $26,000 loan?"

You nod. "When you count in all the interest, that's the way it turns out."

"That sounds like a good arrangement to me," she says. "Of course I'll have to talk to Bob about it. I'll call him tonight and tell him all about your offer."

At this point you say, "That would be good. Tell him all about my offer and see what he says. I'll give you a call in the morning, and you can let me know what you two have decided."

You turn and start for the door. Then you turn back. "On second thought, I'd like to be here when you talk with Bob. He might have questions about my offer, and I'd like to be here to answer them. Could you put in a call to him while he's at work?"

"I suppose I could do that," she says hesitantly.

"If we could come to an agreement on the terms right now, we can set the sale of your house in motion right away. We can get all the legal formalities taken care of quickly, get you and the kids moved to San Diego and get you together with Bob as soon as possible."

This convinces her. She dials the phone and makes her call. She presents your offer to him over the phone, and he seems very interested. He is somewhat hesitant about the terms, especially the no down payment. But she explains, "It's all right, Bob. We'll get the money eventually through the monthly payments. And we'll get *three times* our actual equity in the house after we've received all our monthly payments, because of all the interest. We'll actually be getting about $78,000 for our $26,000 equity."

Your offer is accepted. You feel that you have not only made a good buy in a house, you have also helped to reunite a young family.

11 Bad Tenants For Landlord Equal No Down Payment For You

Any factor which will motivate a property owner to become a highly motivated seller is a factor which will help you greatly in negotiating a no cash down deal with the property owner. One of these factors can be a building full of tenants who are not properly managed, and who are destroying the property, having wild parties, or doing other things which the landlord cannot bear to have happening on his property. Keep an eye out for these situations. You may walk into a no cash down deal.

Suppose you see an apartment building advertised for sale in the newspaper. The phone number listed in the ad is an out of town number.

You call the number and talk with the owner. During your initial conversation, you catch the feeling of distress in the owner's voice and realize that there is a very strong possibility that this individual is a "Don't-Wanter." You follow a line of questioning to see if you are right.

"How long have you owned this particular apartment building?" you ask.

"Oh, about two years now."

"Have you been living out of town and still trying to manage the apartment building here?"

"I tried that in the beginning," he says, a slightly stronger edge of emotion showing in his voice, "but it didn't work. I live too far away. Something was always going wrong and I was constantly making 30 mile trips to try to take care of problems. I'd get calls from the tenants all the time, even in the middle of the night. Something was wrong with the plumbing, or something was wrong with the heating or air conditioner."

He hastens to add, "It was never anything too serious, of course. I could take care of it easily, once I got there. It was just a matter of getting into my car and driving 30 miles to take care of whatever it was, and then driving 30 miles more to get back home. That apartment building is a great deal for anyone who is living nearby."

"Do you live right there in the city?" he asks hopefully.

"Yes," you say. "I live just a few minutes away from that apartment building. I live close enough to it that I could watch over it fairly easily."

Then you add, "You mentioned that you tried to manage the place yourself in the beginning. Does this mean that you have someone else managing it for you right now?"

"Yes," says the man. "I advertised for a manager to live in one of the apartments and manage the whole property. A young fellow answered the ad, and I've had him living there ever since."

"How has that been working out?" you query.

"Well, I don't have so much running around to do this way. But I'm still really too far away to know exactly what is going on in that apartment building. I guess the young fellow is taking care of everything all right."

"Well," you say, "it looks like the next step is for me to take a look at the building. Would you like to be there when I see it, or would you rather have your manager show me through?" You want to see just how much confidence he has in his manager. Does he trust his manager to show you the property, and do a good job of showing you its desirable qualities? Or, does he have little confidence in this manager? Has the manager not really been able to keep things going the way the owner would really like?

"I have to make a trip there to the city this afternoon anyway," the owner replies, "so how about if I meet you there this afternoon about 3:00? Will that be all right?"

"That will be just fine," you say. Now your confidence is growing that your suspicions are being confirmed. This property owner is a real "Don't-Wanter." You can probably negotiate a good no money down deal with him. You agree to meet with him at 3:00.

You show up at the apartment building promptly at 3:00. The owner is already waiting for you.

He introduces himself as Mr. Riley.

With introductions completed, you request a tour of the property.

He gives you a guided tour of the building, pointing out all it's good points. And it is a good building, no question about that.

"It has eight rental units," Mr. Riley says. "Most of them are filled most of the time. I've only been able to rent seven units because I let the manager live free in one unit. But, if you'll be managing the place yourself, you'll be able to rent out all eight."

You respond, "I'll be managing the place myself. Let's see now, how much are you asking for the building, and how much equity do you have in it?"

"It was appraised recently at $96,000. I'll let it go for $90,000 even. There is an assumable mortgage of $44,000 on it. That gives me an equity of $46,000. I'd like a down payment of $8,000 cash."

"Will you take monthly payments on your equity? I'd pay 1% per month on it; that would be $460 a month."

Mr. Riley considers. "That would be all right, I guess. But what about the down payment?"

"To tell you the truth," you say, "I can't really afford that down payment. All I could really afford to do here would be to take over your first mortgage from the bank and start making your payments of $460 a month. I'd take over the building and start managing it, and assume all responsibility. You wouldn't have to worry about what the tenants or your manager doing from then on. It would be my worry, not yours."

You can see that you are getting through to him with this. However, he still looks a little uncertain. You smile at him and say, "And, you'll never get any more phone calls in the middle of the night from your tenants. I promise."

He laughs a little and says, "Okay. You just bought yourself an apartment building."

12   Solving Problems Others Couldn't Solve

Here is the number one principle in what you have to do to avoid negotiations: get people to come to you so you don't have to go out and find them.

You won't find me out on Monday talking to people who put an ad in the newspaper for the first time on Sunday. Once in a while, if I spot a really good deal, I'll be out there talking to the people.

However, my general rule is this: most of the people I talk to about buying their houses have either come to me by themselves, or through a real estate agent on a house that they cannot sell by themselves.

Here is the usual case: the house needs fixing up. The electricity has been turned off, and when people come to see the property, they see a damp, ugly house sitting in the dark with no lights. The place looks scary. It looks like a haunted house. Nobody wants to buy an old, dark, haunted house.

It's easy to become a specialist in buying old houses. You get your earnest money in there, and tie the thing up for 30 days. This gives you time to get the electricity turned on. Then you can start getting bids on it, or sell it, or whatever you want to do with it. Take over those houses that are dark and scary. People are afraid of them.

If you can solve problems in real estate that other people are afraid of, that will be the key to your success. You will be able to measure your success in the future by how many problems you learn to solve today. You get good at solving those problems.

I am not talking to just anybody or everybody who is trying to sell his house at market value and get every dollar possible out of it. I am talking to people who will come in and buy an older house, fix it up, and sell it for a decent profit, but, still at a fair price.

Occasionally, people get in a real bind trying to sell their own houses. *I have had several people who have actually paid me to buy their homes!*

One fellow had a vacant house with monthly payments of $400 on it. It had been sitting idle for nine months! He knew he couldn't sell it because it needed a lot of work and he lacked the means to complete the necessary repairs. As the months went by, he became more and more frustrated.

Finally, he decided that I was his only alternative. He came to me and said, "Wade, all I want is for you to take this thing over. I'm not asking for any down payment on it. I know it needs fixing up and I just can't afford to do it. I'll give you $1,000 in cash right now, if you'll take it off my hands."

I took it. It was really a good deal for me, and he considered it a really good deal for himself.

He considered me his only alternative. Why was this? This is because I have gotten my name up in front of so many people, so many agents, and so many investors, that they all call me about the houses that they can't handle themselves.

Now consider this for a moment. Which side of the fence would you rather be on? Would you rather have them dictating the terms to you? Or would you rather be in the position of dictating the terms to them? If you go to them, they may end up dictating the terms to you. But, if they come to you, this gives you a real opportunity to dictate the terms you want. They are now in a position where they are going to listen to you very intently. And, chances are, they will accept your offer.

Don't get me wrong. This may be tough for you in the beginning. Doing all that's necessary to get your name in front of people may be tough.

But once you position yourself, you'll have a real place in the market. You can get yourself into a situation where people are calling you regularly. You become a dominant force in the market place. You can become the "firstest with the mostest" in your own locale.

If you get your name up in front of people, and get those agents working for you, then you may end up buying five, ten, or fifteen houses every year from one agent. When this happens, that agent is going to call you every time he has a good deal on his hands. That agent is really going to work for you. You have positioned yourself with that agent, and he sees you more and more as his major source of funds. You are his source for getting the job done on houses that cannot be sold.

While you are becoming his major source of funds, he is in the process of becoming your major source of funds. This is a great win/win situation for both you and the agent.

However, do not rely on the agent alone. Keep your name in front of everybody. Let them know that you are the one who will solve the problems other people can't solve. Make it clear that you are the one person in the area who is most likely to buy an old house which had problems that other people can't solve.

You will have a flood of people coming to see you, asking you to buy their houses. That puts you in a great position to tell them under what terms you will consider buying their property.

This is a powerful position for you to be in.

Assuming The
Seller's Obligations

13

The general principle here is this: whenever any seller asks for a large chunk of cash as a down payment on his property, your job is to find out *why* he wants that large chunk of money. Once you find out the reason, you can go to work and figure out what to do about it.

Here is an example of a special case that arises quite frequently. You will find many people who are in debt, and are trying to solve their debt problems by asking for large down payments, in cash, on the properties they are trying to sell. In other words, they are trying to use large chunks of your cash to pay off their own debts.

Here is how you can handle the situation very effectively, taking care of the seller's debts, and still getting a good deal on his property:

You find a nice house for sale in a nice neighborhood. You walk inside and start talking with the owner.

You walk around the house with him, looking over everything very carefully. You don't say anything while you are looking. You just look carefully, and be sure you let him see you looking at everything carefully.

Finally, you say to him, "How much are you asking for your house, Mr. Krebbs?"

"Well," he says, "it was appraised a couple of months ago at $65,000." You see that he is looking at you to see how the price strikes you. You maintain a non-committal look on your face.

"Of course," he adds, "I might be willing to lower the price a little, if I could get a quick sale."

You look at him and nod. "If a quick sale is what you want, I'm your man, if you lower the price far enough. How much would you be willing to lower the price, Mr. Krebbs?"

The seller seems a little distraught. He is trying to figure out how low he is going to have to go to get you to buy his property. You can see the uncertainty in his face. You have learned to always watch the sellers' faces, to try to see how they are thinking about things.

"How about $55,000?" asks Mr. Krebbs.

"That sounds like a good deal," you reply. "I'll take you up on that, Mr. Krebbs, on one condition."

"What's that?" he asks a little excitedly. He sees that you are responding to his offer, and that you will actually buy his house if he can meet this one condition. He is very eager to know what this one condition is.

"No down payment," you say. "I'll take over your mortgage, give you a second mortgage, and give you monthly payments for your equity in the place."

"But, I *need* a $10,000 down payment in cash!" he exclaims. "I've got to have $10,000 in cash!"

"What do you need $10,000 for?" you ask. "Is there something special you need that money for right now?"

"Yes!" he exclaims agitatedly. "I'm $10,000 in debt! My only hope of getting out of debt is to sell the house and get enough cash from it to pay off my debt. Otherwise, I've got no way in the world to pay off that debt."

"I can handle your debt," you say.

"What? How?"

"There are two ways I can do it," you explain. "The first way is this. I can contact your creditor and assume full liability for your debt. Is your debt a lump sum, or are you making monthly payments on it?"

"I've been making monthly payments on it up until now. I thought that when I sold the house I could pay it all off in one lump sum."

"How much are the monthly payments?" you ask.

"$100 a month," he says.

"Fine," you say. "I'll take over that loan, and start paying that $100 a month myself. And we'll just deduct that $10,000 from the selling price of the house, and then I'll owe you $40,000 for the house."

"Yes, that should work. But, you mentioned a second way. What is the second way?"

"The second way is this," you explain. "You keep on making your monthly payments of $100 to your creditor, and I will give you a note for $10,000, and start paying $100 a month to you. You can have your choice. Which way would you prefer?"

The seller considers. "I just want to be clear out of it. I would rather you just go ahead and assume the loan."

"Great!" you say. "Then we have a deal?"

"We've got a deal," Mr. Krebbs says, looking really relieved for the first time since your arrival.

Note: the seller might want security on the note you are giving him. You can always give this to him in the form of a third mortgage on the house you are buying from him.

14 Down Payment In Monthly Payments

One day you discover a charming house in a favorable neighborhood. You see that this place has real possibilities as you are talking to the owner about buying the house. "What kind of terms would you give me on buying your home, Mrs. Lawton?"

She says, with no hesitation, "I've got to have $8,000 down in cash."

The seller is asking $50,000 for the house, and you know that the house is worth at least this much, so you do want to buy the property from her, but you just do not have $8,000 in cash you can spend on a down payment. You offer, "I can see that the house is worth what you are asking, Mrs. Lawton, but I just don't have $8,000 cash right now."

She looks very disappointed. "Oh, I guess that's it then." She starts to walk you to the door. As you are walking beside her, you say, "There might be a way we could work something out."

"I doubt it," she says. "If you don't have the $8,000, I don't possibly see what you could do."

You respond, "Why don't we do this? I can't pay you $8,000 right now in one huge lump sum, but I could pay you that $8,000 in several smaller chunks, a month at a time!"

The seller looks at you suspiciously. "One month at a time? How long would it take before I had the whole $8,000?"

"Well," you say, "we could do it one of two ways. You can have your choice. The first way is, I'll be taking over your first mortgage with the bank, and making the monthly payments directly to them. I'll also be giving you a second mortgage on your home for your equity, and, I'll be making you the monthly payments on that. In order to pay you off your $8,000, I could just increase the amount of my monthly payments to you by $200 a month, and keep paying that extra $200 a month every month until I have paid you the full $8,000."

"And what is the second way?" she asks.

"The second way is this. I can pay off that full $8,000 a month at a time, over a period of twelve months. I'll divide that $8,000 into twelve chunks and pay you off one chunk at a time. But in order for me to do this, I would have to ask you for a moratorium on your monthly mortgage payments during the first year. Which way would you rather go?"

She thinks for a moment and finally says, "I think I'd like the way where you pay off the whole $8,000 in one year. I'd get my money sooner that way."

"Do we have a sale, then?" you ask.

She smiles at you. "Yes, Mr. Taylor. Under these conditions, we have a sale."

Note: if the down payment is fairly large in comparison with the regular monthly payments you will be making on your mortgage to the seller, the seller may prefer to have the large down payment paid off during the course of a year in preference to receiving any monthly mortgage payments. However, if the mortgage payments are sizeable compared with the down payment, the seller will probably opt for the addition of $200 or so dollars a month added on to the regular monthly mortgage. Just put the question to the seller, and let them choose. People like to be in the driver's seat, making their own choices. It is also a good idea to give the seller a chance to think things over and consider the relative value of the large down payment being paid off sooner, as compared to receiving the regular monthly mortgage payments every month with a $200 bonus added every month until the down payment is paid off.

Giving people choices is enjoyable and it works!

15

Lease With
Option To Buy

Here is a *very* effective technique for buying a house with no cash down. This is based on the fact that in many cases, you discover that you can actually *lease* a property for less money per month than you would have to pay in monthly payments if you bought the property outright. Whenever you find a case like this, lease the property with an option to buy. One of your big advantages here is that you will not actually be buying the property now, but some time in the future, and you will be paying today's prices! No matter how much the property goes up in value, by the time you actually buy it, you will be paying the price which had been set today. You will receive all that appreciation in the property, even though you have not owned the property during the time of your lease.

Let's look at an example. You are scanning through the newspaper and you come across an ad which says RENT OR LEASE WITH OPTION TO BUY—SINGLE FAMILY HOME. You call the owner on the phone and go out to inspect the property.

You find the place in a fairly nice section of town, and the house itself is presentable. You would not mind if you lived there yourself. Whenever you look at a property, you have learned to look at it as though you were the one who is going to be living there, either renting or buying it.

Introductions are concluded; you go inside and look the place over. It is a fairly nice home for a rental, but it is vacant now. You know that this property would rent reasonably for $600 a month in the prevailing rental market for this area.

"I'm asking $500 a month rent for the house," says Mr. Mitchell. "I could get more, I know, but, I've lowered the rent to make it a really good deal."

You realize that this place has been vacant for awhile, and Mr. Mitchell is trying desperately to rent it. That is why he has lowered the rent by $100 a month. You know that you can negotiate with an owner/landlord like this.

"Has the place been vacant long?" you inquire.

"Oh, for a while," he admits. He seems somewhat disturbed by the question.

"I guess that when you rent it out by the month, you can expect it to be vacant at least a couple of months out of the year, right? That seems to be about average with month by month rentals."

"Yes," says Mr. Mitchell, "I guess it is."

"So in this case, two months rent would be $1,000. You could expect to lose at least $1,000 rent every year because of vacancies, right?"

The owner shrugs wearily. "I guess that's about right."

"So you are really getting about $5,000 a year rental on this place, instead of $6,000. $5,000 divided by twelve months equals, (you work this out on your little pocket calculator) approximately $417. This means that $417 a month is what you are really averaging when you rent this place month to month." You show him the figures on your little calculator.

"I'll tell you what I'll do," you say. "I'm willing to rent your house, not just month by month, but on a long-term loan lease, if you're willing to give me a discount. Since you wouldn't be having to worry about vacancies any longer, we could just drop the monthly payments down to $417 per month, then you would be getting your average monthly rental which you actually receive in the long run, when you count the two months out of every year that your house just stands here vacant. And, you'll be able to count on the money coming in every month, without any sudden gaps in between. Wouldn't you rather be able to have $417 a month that you could count on as a sure thing, than to just average that much over the course of the year, never knowing when your income will just suddenly stop?"

Mr. Mitchell sighs, "Yes, I think I would."

"There's another thing," you continue, "when tenants move out of a house, how do they leave it? Is it always as clean as you would like? Do you ever have repairs to make after the tenants move out? Tenants who just move out suddenly can really leave horrible situations behind them. And how much is all this going to cost you?"

You could tell from the look on Mr. Mitchell's face that he is remembering vividly some of these horrible situations, and how much they have cost him in the past. "It does cost," he agrees.

"I won't do that to you," you promise, "because I want to lease this house long term. I won't be moving out on you. So you won't be having to take care of all these added expenses that occur when the tenants move out. I'll tell you what I'll do; I'll even take care of the basic maintenance. You won't have to be bothered with those expenses or pestered with the grief of managing this property. I'll take care of all the problems, if you'll give me some additional discount."

"How much of a discount are you talking about?" he asks.

"If you let me lease this place at $375 a month, I'll sign a lease for seven years and take care of all the maintenance. I'll do this if you'll give me an option to buy this place at the end of that time and give me the right to rent the place out to other tenants during those seven years. Remember, I'll be responsible for the tenants and everything they do. I'll be responsible for keeping up the place and taking care of all the maintenance. You won't have to do any of the managing; I'll take care of it all."

"You want an option to buy?" asks the seller. "The appraised price on this house is $60,000. Are you willing to pay that price?"

"Yes," you assure him. "I'll pay $60,000 for this place, and I'll put it in writing right in the lease with the option to buy contract."

"What kind of terms would you want?" asks Mr. Mitchell.

You look him straight in the eye. "I'll sign the contract to pay you $60,000 cash for this place at the end of seven years. Of course, I would want the right to exercise this option any time during the seven years."

Mr. Mitchell's jaw drops appreciably. "$60,000 cash? You'll sign a contract to pay me $60,000 all in cash for this place?"

You smile at him. "That's exactly right," you assure him. $60,000 all in cash."

This is the finishing touch, as far as the owner is concerned. He extends his hand to shake yours. "I'll take it," he says.

What have you just done? You have just bought a $60,000 house, and income property for no cash down. You have promised to pay the owner $60,000 cash in the future by the time those seven years are up. This house will have appreciated greatly in value, and you'll have no trouble at all in refinancing, and obtaining the cash needed to pay off the owner in one lump sum. If he already has a mortgage with a bank, you could just assume that mortgage, and refinance on the equity to pay the owner back his equity. By the end of the seven years, you will still have a great deal of equity left over after you do this.

In the meantime, you have a good income property. If you get out there and manage that house, you can rent it out to other tenants at the regular rental value of the house, which is actually $500 a month. You are paying the owner $375 a month so this will give you an income of $125 a month. If you manage well, this will be a good income property for you.

Probably at any time after three years from your signing this contract, the house will have appreciated enough in value so that you would be able to refinance it and receive more than enough money to buy the house from the owner.

Also, any time during those seven years of your contract, you would have the right to resell this house at a higher price to a new buyer and bring in a profit on the sale of the house.

16 Getting The Down Payment From Real Estate Agents

In a typical money machine deal (see my book *Real Estate Money Machine*), you will buy a house at a price of $42,000, and the seller wants a down payment of $2,000. The house has a $30,000 first mortgage on it, so the seller has an equity of $12,000 in the house.

Now, let's take a good look at this $2,000 down payment. Just where is that $2,000 down payment going to go?

Do you know how much commission the real estate agent is going to make on this sale? That commission is going to be in the order of $2,500.

That is really where your $2,000 down payment is going to go! The seller of the house is going to get to touch your $2,000 for just a few minutes, and then he is going to have to kiss it goodbye and give it all to the real estate agent for that commission, plus about $500 of his own money.

Once you know where the money from your down payment is going, what can you do about it?

This is what I did. I started calling real estate agents on the phone and explained that I had thought of a new way of paying their commissions. I even took one out to lunch.

After he had eaten well (at my expense), I started talking to him about my new idea. I said, "You've got a 7% commission coming to you on every house you sell, right? And that's supposed to come from the seller, not the buyer. Well, I want to buy houses through you, and I'm willing to pay you that 7% commission for every house I buy."

He wasn't used to a buyer offering to pay his commission. I went on. "For every house I buy through you, I will give you a mortgage secured against that house. Each mortgage will be for the amount of your commission, and, I will pay you 11% interest on that mortgage at a monthly payment rate of 1% of the total amount every month. If the commission is $1,800, I will pay you $18 a month for the whole course of the loan."

He sat there full of my good food and said, "*No!*"

But the following morning, my phone rang, and it was the real estate agent who had said "No!" the day before. He had been thinking my offer over, slept on it, and had called me up this morning to say "*Yes!*"

This was also going to be a very profitable deal for both of us!

When I pay him one month at a time, he gets to claim the payments on his taxes at a monthly rate. If the agent is willing to receive his commissions over the entire course of the loan, he can claim his profits over that extended period.

This was the beginning of a very profitable deal for both of us.

I bought a house through him, and he had a $2,800 commission coming. He was willing to accept monthly installment payments from me. He needed cash a couple of months later, so he took my mortgage and sold it to one of those companies that buy mortgages at a discount. He received $1,600 cash from the mortgage. He sold it at a discount, but he had $1,600 cash in his pocket that he would not have had if I had not been able to afford to buy that house through him. He had also received two monthly installments from me.

I bought another house through him and gave him an $1,800 mortgage on it. He took my mortgage and gave it to his attorney to pay off a $1,400 attorney fee with it!

Later, he took two more of my notes which totaled $5,000 and he used them to buy a $4,000 Mercedes!

Then, he took three more of my notes that totaled $10,000 and used them as a down payment on four four-plexes!

Then he wanted to buy a $130,000 house for himself. The seller wanted $10,000 down in cash. My real estate agent gave the seller $11,000 in my mortgage notes for the down payment.

That agent was out there having a ball with my mortgage notes! He was using my mortgage notes for *money*! He was out trading my notes for things he wanted to buy. When someone wanted a big cash payment for something, what did he do? He gave them one or more of my notes, enough to total the amount of cash wanted by the seller.

Talk about making money! I created my own money and it was all legal.

17 Seller Pays The Real Estate Commission Out Of His Equity, Not His Cash

Let's stop and take a good look at this situation. Who is really paying these commissions? Where is this money really coming from? The seller's equity! That's what it's all about! It's the equity in all those houses you're buying that makes your "money really worth something!"

All I am really doing here is selling off a small part of the equity in each one of the houses I buy. I give a little of this equity to the real estate agent in the form of a mortgage note and whenever he wants to buy something, he just passes my mortgage notes along to the seller, and the seller takes them in place of money.

Let's look at our example. I bought a house for $42,000 with a $2,000 down payment. It has a $30,000 first mortgage on it. $42,000 minus $30,000 leaves $12,000 in equity that belongs to the seller. I owe the seller $2,000 for the down payment. The seller owes the real estate agent $2,500 for his commission.

I go to the seller and say, "You have $12,000 in equity in this house. I am giving you a cash down payment of $2,000. That leaves you with $10,000 equity. But, you owe the real estate agent $2,500 for his commission fee. I'll pay that $2,500 to the real estate agent and take that out of your equity. Wouldn't you rather pay the real estate agent out of your equity than out of your cash?"

In this way, we always take the commissions out of the seller's equity instead of the cash he receives for the down payment. Would any seller rather pay commissions out of equity or out of his own cash?

Equity! Equity by all means!

Now, let's look at these two notes I'm paying off. I am paying off a note of $2,500 to the real estate agent at a rate of 1% per month. That payment is $25 a month. The other note is a $7,500 mortgage note to the seller of the house from his equity. I am paying that off at 1% per month, so my monthly payment there is $75. This adds up to a total of $100 per month I am paying to the real estate agent and to the seller of the house.

Just how much extra does it cost to do this? Two first class postage stamps. The seller is happy because he sold his house and he didn't have to pay the real estate agent's commission out of his own cash, but out of his equity. The real estate agent is happy because he sold a house and is getting a commission, even though it is in monthly installments. And, he is getting *interest* on that commission. You have made a banker out of him, too.

I am happy because I have just gotten a great deal on buying this house. I paid only $2,000 down on a $42,000 house. This is less than 5% down.

This is a win/win/win situation for the seller, the real estate agent, and for the most important part of this triad, *me*!

18   Selling The Option Back To The Seller

One day, you find a good rental house, a single-family dwelling near the center of town. It is near the schools, near the shopping center, and looks as though it would be good either to keep as a rental, or to resell for a profit. You walk into the house and meet the owner, a Mrs. Donahue, a trim, grey haired lady.

"How much are you asking for you home, Mrs. Donahue?"

"$60,000," she replies.

"Does it have an assumable mortgage?" you ask.

"Yes," she replies. "It has an assumable mortgage of $34,000."

"Then that gives you an equity of $26,000. Will you take monthly payments on your equity? I'll assume your mortgage with the bank and give you a second mortgage on that equity. That would be $260 a month."

"How about a down payment?" she asks.

You hesitate. "How much of a down payment are you talking about?"

"I'd like a down payment of $6,000," she says mildly, but firmly.

$6,000! You don't have $6,000 to spare. You don't have $6,000 in cash at all! What are you going to do here?

Here's the answer. You say, "$6,000 is a lot of cash, Mrs. Donahue. I don't have that much cash right now, but maybe we can still work something out."

You start looking around at the house. "The house is in very good condition, isn't it?"

"Of course it is," she replies crisply. "I always keep any property of mine in the best condition possible."

You agree. "And this is a pretty good neighborhood, isn't it? Close to the shopping centers and the schools?"

"Yes, it is. None of my tenants have ever complained either about the house or about the neighborhood. They have all been quite content about living here."

You look around at the house thoughtfully. Then you say, "What about the property values in this neighborhood? Have they been going up steadily in the last few years?"

She nods firmly. "Yes. I've been watching the property values closely. They have been going up every year around here, at least 10 or 12% a year."

"And you expect the property values to keep on going up in this neighborhood at the same rate?"

She nods again. "Of course they are going to keep on going up. They have been going up for years and years, and they are going to continue to keep going up."

"Why are you selling the house, then? Are you getting tired of managing it as a rental?"

"Well, yes I am. I've managed the house for some years now, and the truth is I am a little tired of managing a rental."

"All right, then. I'd like to buy this house from you and take the management completely off your hands. You would have no responsibility from then on because I would be buying the house from you. But how would you like to stay in for a percentage of the house? I can just sell you back an option to buy 10% of the value of this house. I'll sell you 10% of the interest in the house in exchange for that $6,000 down payment.

"How would that work?" she asks.

"This means that if I ever resell this house to a new buyer, you will get 10% of the profit. You say the property values here are appreciating from 10 to 12% every year, right?"

"That's right," she affirms readily.

"Then, if I sell this house five years from now, it should be worth, (you pull out your pocket calculator and multiply the $60,000 by 1.1, then the result of that multiplication by 1.1 again and so on, until you have made the multiplication five times) a total of $96,360. Now I subtract $60,000 and that gives me $36,630. Ten percent is $3,663.

You look at her and say, "That $3,663 would be your share of the profit."

"Of course, if I sold it at the end of six years, your profit would be, (you calculate rapidly on your calculator), $4,629."

You look at her and smile. "Would you like to stay in for 10% of the profit? That can be my $6,000 down payment."

Her face is set, and you know that she has made up her mind, one way or the other.

"I'll stay in for 10% of the profit. You can forget the down payment."

Get one of those small cheap pocket calculators and carry it with you in your pocket. Learn how to do this simple multiplication. If the property is going up 10% in value every year, then at the end of the year, it is going to be worth 110% of what is was in the beginning. 110% is the same as 1.1. Follow through this example:

Year One: $60,000 times 1.1 equals $66,000
Year Two: $66,000 times 1.1 equals $72,000
Year Three: $72,000 times 1.1 equals $79,000
Year Four: $79,000 times 1.1 equals $87,846.
Year Five: $87,846 times 1.1 equals $96,630.60
Year Six: $96,630.60 times 1.1 equals $106,293.66
Year Seven: $106,293.66 times 1.1 equals $116,923.02
Year Eight: $116,923.02 times 1.1 equals $128,625.32

In each case, subtract $60,000 from the new value of the house, and the result will be your profit on the house if you sell it at the end of the year.

Carry this calculator with you wherever you go. As you start multiplying 1.1 times the value of the house, you will see the home owner's eyes bulge larger and larger as the results become greater and greater.

We used 10% in this example. If the down payment asked by the owner is a larger percent of the sale price of the house, then offer the owner a larger percentage of the profit when you sell the house.

If you offer the owner 20% of the profit, then you will be multiplying the value of his house times 1.2 when you are demonstrating the yearly profits to him. If you offer him 30% of the profit you will be multiplying each year by 1.3, and so on.

Selling the buyer back an option on his own house can be a very effective way of completely nullifying that cash down payment!

Section 3

The
Seller
Accepts
Monthly
Payments

The Seller Accepts Monthly Payments

How do you talk people out of wanting cash for the equity in their property? How do you talk them into not only accepting monthly payments, but actually desiring monthly payments in preference to a large chunk of cash all at once?

Someone walks into the seller's house, appraises it, and says, "Sir, you have $20,000 equity in your house."

Before that seller ever gets his cash, what do you suppose he has already done with it inside his brain? He has already spent every dime of that money!

Then you come walking into his house and say, "I'm willing to give you $20,000 for the equity in your house. But, I can't give it to you all at once. I can only give it to you at $200 a month."

What happens inside the seller's brain at this point? You have just shattered all his dreams!

They have the desired results set up solidly in their minds. Then you come walking in and start talking about monthly payments. The instant they hear the words "monthly payments," their first impulse is to throw you out of their house! They look upon you as an unspeakable real estate bandit who is plotting to rob them of their cherished dreams.

How are you going to talk your way out of a situation like this? There are several very effective ways of dealing with this situation.

One way is to read the FOR SALE ads in the newspaper everyday, and whenever a new one appears in the paper, call the number, talk to the seller, and see if you would really be interested in buying the property, before you look at it.

Another way of accomplishing this is to *advertise*. You place your own advertisement in the newspaper, and people know that you are in the market to buy houses. People will be trying to contact you instead of you having to contact them.

To talk people out of taking all cash, educate them about it. To them, this is monthly income and it is something that people get to like, knowing they can depend on it for many years to come. You can save tons of money this way.

Also, you can be successful in buying real estate with no money down by making the sellers like you and trust you. This is especially true when you are negotiating the final contract. The first goal you should have when you are talking with the seller of a property is to establish trust and credibility with him.

Always remember this: people like you because you show an interest in them. It's that simple!

Remember to *never criticize* the person's property!

Point of fact, if you actually appraise the property's good points, or it's furnishings, you can work real wonders in creating a positive emotional environment. If people can see that you appreciate their home, and the things they have done to make it a comfortable home, they will have a warm, friendly feeling toward you. In their hearts, they will desire you to be the one who is going to buy their home.

The Desirability Of A Steady Monthly Income

19

I bought a house a couple of years ago for $45,000, with a $30,000 loan from the sellers, $320 monthly payments, and a four year balloon payment at the end. That loan is two years old now. Two years from now the whole $30,000 is due. Does this sound like something you would like to do, have to dig up $30,000 in two years?

I went back to the seller and told him, "I really don't want to have to pay this $30,000 in two years."

The seller said, "Why don't you just keep making the monthly payments?"

I was very agreeable to that! (*relieved*, too.) I said, "That's okay." Then I asked him, "Why did you want the $30,000 balloon in the first place?"

He replied, "This real estate agent I knew told me to make you that offer."

But he had grown to like those monthly payments.

When this happens, you can just type up this new amendment on the original document, then go and officially rerecord the original document with the changes written into it. Or, an attorney can type up whole new agreement and have that recorded.

20 Always Make The Seller Feel Secure

Have you ever been out talking to an elderly couple about buying their home?

What do they want? They want cash!

I was out one day talking with a couple in their seventies. They were both in poor health. They had been living in this house for over 20 years and the property had become run down. After I bought the place from them, I had to put three coats of paint on it. The house just sucked in the paint.

Initially, when I talked to them about buying the house they wanted $40,000 for it. I could see that it would be $60,000 or $70,000, if it were really fixed up right.

I went ahead and offered them the $40,000 they asked, but told them I would like to pay them off at $400 a month.

They told me this. "We would personally like to have $400 a month. That would really help us with our retirement. But, we think we should ask for $40,000 cash, so we can give it to our children. We have four children, and we would like very much to give each one of them $10,000."

I asked, "What do you think your children are going to do with all this money?"

They replied, "They will probably blow it. All except for David."

I said, "How about this? I will go ahead and give you $400 a month for as long as you both live, and if and when you die, I will give each one of your children $100 a month for the balance of the loan."

When elderly people reach that stage of their lives, they have a great desire to be loved and remembered when they are gone. If the children get all the money in one lump sum, what is going to happen to that money? The money is soon going to be spent. Are the elderly people going to be loved and remembered for that money very long?

But if I am going to be paying each one of their children $100 a month for the next 20 years, what is going to happen then? Every time that monthly check for $100 comes to them, those children are going to remember their parents.

Am I fulfilling a great need in those elderly people's lives? The answer is obvious.

Elderly people understand better than anyone the value of this program. They can retire on a good steady monthly income, and when they are gone, their children can have a regular monthly income that keeps them in remembrance of their parents.

Occasionally, you may be on the receiving end of this negative argument. When I talk to people about paying them $200 a month instead of giving them $20,000 in one lump sum, some people are going to say, "Hold, it Mr. Cook. Just how much do you think this $200 a month is going to be worth twenty years from now?" They want to know the value of that money twenty years down the road.

I reply, "I honestly don't know. Maybe $200 a month will be only worth a Chicken McNugget. But if that is the case, then what is $20,000 going to be worth 20 years from now, if it's spent right now? Do you see my point? If it's gone now, then it's not going to be worth anything 20 years from now. Are Chicken McNuggets worth more than nothing?"

21

Get Them
What They Want

I found a nice house which was owned by a lady who was buying another property on a VA loan. She wanted a huge down payment on the place she was selling.

I offered her a small down payment, but she wanted much more.

She said, "No, no, no! I've got to have cash! I want to buy furniture for my new home."

I said, "How much furniture do you want to buy for your new house?" She wanted to furnish the entire home.

I said, "Why don't you go down to the store and pick out everything you want, and see how much the total amount comes to?"

Now, I had already made her an offer in which I was going to pay her $375 a month in payments. When she went down to that furniture store and picked out all the furniture she wanted, we discovered that the furniture store would let her buy all that furniture on monthly payments of $345 a month.

I said, "You don't need all that cash at once to buy that furniture. You can buy it from the furniture store at $345 a month. I'm offering to make you monthly payments of $375 a month. What's more, my payments of $375 a month are going to be coming to you for the next 25 years! In three or four years you will have paid off the furniture, and you'll still have my checks for $375 a month coming into you for the next umpteen years!"

She got the point! I got the house, and she got the furniture!

This lady was really happy. I had not given her the huge chunk of cash she had wanted originally, but I had gotten her what she *really* wanted—that beautiful set of furniture to furnish her brand new house. More than that, she was going to have my monthly payments coming to her for many years. She would be free to spend that money on whatever she wanted to spend it on.

As long as you can get people what they really want, they will be every bit as happy as if you had given them all the money in a lump sum which they asked for in the beginning. The reason these people ask for that big down payment of cash in the beginning is they are so cash oriented they can't think of any other way of getting what they want.

However, you can often change their minds by showing them how you can get them what they really want, but in a different way than using that large chunk of cash.

The principle is this: solve their cash problems with monthly payments!

Always point out that in the long run, they will get three times as much money because of the interest you are paying as part of your regular monthly payment.

Making A Wealthy Banker Out Of The Seller 22

When you start making these monthly payments to the seller, and these monthly payments are going to continue for years, you are actually making a successful banker out of the seller.

This money does not pay off quickly. We have established that in the long run the seller will make more money for his equity than he ever would if he had received all cash at once.

You can go to the seller and tell him something like this: "Mr. Jones, I know that you need your $20,000 right now. I know that you've made commitments with that money. If I gave you your whole $20,000 right now, what is not spent will end up in the pocket of the IRS. But if I gave you this money at a rate of $200 a month, in seven or eight years, I will have paid you your whole $20,000 and I'll still owe you about $19,999 on your loan to me!"

This is because interest income is by far the largest part of the loan which is being paid off in the early years.

You could get an amortization schedule from a bank and show the seller exactly what he is going to receive, every year, right to the penny. Also, it will show what the balance of his loan to you is going to be at the end of each year and more importantly, just how much money is rolling into him annually from this loan!

You can tell him, "In the seven or eight years to follow, I will have paid you another $20,000, and I'll still owe you about $13,000."

A look at the amortization schedule tells the story. A transaction like this will let him become a banker, with all the same rights and privileges.

When you call him a banker, how do you think he will react? Do you think he is going to frown at that? Not by a long-shot.

23 My Special "Secret Weapon"

My "secret weapon" is this: enthusiasm and excitement. With these tools, I have been able to enhance the odds of the seller agreeing to do business on a no money down, monthly payment basis.

A newspaper columnist who writes a real estate column said, "Wade, you mentioned something that is most important to anyone's success. I don't know if anyone else caught it, but I did. *Your excitement is what carries the day!*"

It's true! I *love* monthly payments! I take them all the time. I would much rather have monthly payments coming in to me every month instead of a large sum of cash.

You don't need cash in buying real estate. *Monthly payments will pay the bills.*

The bills come in to you each month. How are you going to pay them? Monthly payments are all you need in order to retire. Big chunks of cash just disappear.

What you really need is to build up a good stockpile of monthly payments coming to you! Then, if you feel like retiring, you can just go ahead and retire on the income from the monthly payments. This is a source of real security.

Blanket Mortgage To Make The Seller Feel Secure 24

You have just found a great house in a nice neighborhood! Everything about the property is right.

Inside the house you are talking with the owner, Mr. Jarvis. "All right, Mr. Jarvis. You're selling the house for $65,000, and you have a $35,000 mortgage on it with the bank, right?"

The seller, a middle-aged man with slightly graying hair, says, "That's right. So I'll want $30,000 for my equity."

"Will you take monthly payments for your equity?" By this time, you are quite used to asking the question, and you are used to having the question answered one way or the other. It doesn't bother you so much now when an owner says, "No."

You know by this time that if you ask enough owners, some of them are going to say "Yes!"

Mr. Jarvis says, "Yes." He'd be willing to take monthly payments. But he would like a sizable enough down payment to get you into the house.

He goes on, "First of all, how much are you willing to pay in the way of monthly payments?"

You respond, "I'll pay 1% of the principle per month, and 1% of $30,000 is $300. So I would be paying you $300 per month in monthly payments. I can pay you 9% interest on it, and we'll amortize the whole loan at 9%."

You have learned you can set up any loan, any time, any place by deciding how large your monthly payments should be, deciding on a set interest rate, and then just amortizing the loan by the table, using the interest rate. This will determine how many years or months the loan will take until it is completely paid off.

Mr. Jarvis says, "Nine percent is pretty close. Would you go for 10%? I've got to have at least 10% interest."

"All right," you say, "I'll buy it at 10%."

"Now, the only thing left that still bothers me is this. I'm all set up to sell this house. I've advertised it and done the leg work on it. You're here now, and you want to buy now. So if I sell it to you, and take it off the market, suppose you are able to make the payments for a few months, and suddenly something happens and you can't make the payments anymore. What happens to me then? I'd have to go through foreclosure and take the house back. Then, I would have to go through everything all over again to sell the house."

He is pacing softly back and forth across the room as he is talking. "I don't really need a lot of cash for a down payment. I don't really need that money. *But,*" he eyes you pointedly, "if you pay me $5,000 in cash as a down payment, I can be sure just how serious you will be in continuing to make the monthly payments. I'll be $5,000 sure. Do you see what I mean?"

"Yes, I see what you mean."

The seller continues, "If I let you come in with no down payment at all and just take over the payments of my mortgage to the bank and start making payments to me on a second mortgage, based on my equity, then you won't really be into the house a dime's worth, except for your monthly payments. You could be renting the house out, and using it as a source of income. But, if anything went wrong you could just walk away from the whole deal, and leave me sitting here with the house again. I'd be back where I started from. I couldn't live with that kind of arrangement. Before I sell my house to you, I've got to be absolutely sure that you will continue to make your monthly payments and I'll never have to foreclose on you. Do you follow my line of reasoning?"

"I read you clearly," you say, "and if that's what's bothering you, I think I have a solution for it. It's called a 'blanket mortgage.' I'll be giving you a second mortgage on this house to cover the amount of your equity. If I should stop making your monthly payments, you can foreclose and take your house back. You'll have your house back, but nothing else from me except monthly payments. But, with a blanket mortgage, I will include something else under that same mortgage besides your house."

"That sounds interesting," says Mr. Jarvis. "What did you have in mind? What would you be willing and able to include under this blanket mortgage besides my house?"

At this point, you think over every single thing you own in this world that the seller might accept for additional collateral under this blanket mortgage.

You say, "Well, I own a nice lot over on the other side of town. I'm paying it off on a mortgage to the bank, but I have $2,500 of equity in it. Would you like me to include that under the blanket mortgage?"

"That would help," says Mr. Jarvis. "But even so . . . I'd like something more. You might not be too distressed by the loss of that particular lot."

Then he says, "Do you have anything else you could put under this blanket mortgage?"

"Well," you admit slowly, "I do own my own home. I still have a pretty good sized mortgage on it."

Mr. Jarvis looks very interested. "How much equity do you have in your home?"

"I have about $8,000 worth in it right now."

The seller smiles in satisfaction. "Your own home will do very nicely. If you include your own home under this blanket mortgage, along with my house, I can be absolutely certain you are not going to walk away from the arrangement. I'll know that if you stop making payments to me on my house, I can take back not only my property, but your home as well. I have a great deal of confidence that you would make every effort to make your monthly payments to me if the alternative is that you lose your own home. So I will be quite content to hold a blanket mortgage including this house I am selling you, and your own home. You can consider this transaction successfully closed."

"All right," you say. "It's a deal."

This seller is one shrewd customer. He will never sell you his house until he is absolutely sure that you would have a great deal to lose by walking out on the deal. He is both intelligent and suspicious.

However, he is a highly reasonable man. When he sees that you are willing to legally place your own home under this blanket mortgage along with his house, he feels secure that you will always make your monthly payments to him.

The blanket mortgage is a highly effective instrument for making a suspicious seller feel secure.

Understanding The Seller's Needs

25

You have found a nice house for sale, and you have inspected it thoroughly enough to determine there is nothing wrong with it. The seller seems flexible. As you're talking to him you say, "$60,000 seems like a fair price for your house, Mr. Thomas. What kind of terms can you give me on it? Will you take monthly payments from me for your equity?"

Mr. Thomas shakes his head solemnly. "No, I'm afraid not. I'm going to need all cash on this deal."

"How much is your equity?" you ask.

"$20,000," he replies. "And I need it all in cash."

You know that this house has a fair market value of at least $65,000, and, that Mr. Thomas has deliberately dropped the price $5,000 in order to get a quick sale. You know he needs this cash for something, or at least he thinks he needs all this cash for something.

You come right out and ask him, "How do you intend to use all that $20,000, Mr. Thomas?"

"I am moving to a new home, and I need that $20,000 to buy the equity in that other home."

You nod understandingly. "Oh, I see. In other words, Mr. Thomas, it isn't really the $20,000 you need. What you really need is to be able to buy your new home. Is that right?"

He looks a little surprised.

"Mr. Thomas, I know a lot of techniques for buying houses without using cash. All you really need are the monthly payments. If I buy your house from you, even though I won't be paying you any money down, I will be making these monthly payments to you regularly, every month. You can use these monthly payments to buy the owner's equity in the new home you will be buying. I pay you every month, and you turn around and pay him every month."

"Well," says Mr. Thomas, "if this will really work, then I wouldn't really need that $20,000 all in cash. But, I don't know what the owner of the other house would say if I just offer him monthly payments on his equity."

You smile at the seller and say, "Let me go with you to talk to the owner. By the time I'm finished explaining all the benefits of paying monthly payments instead of huge cash down payments, I think he will be happy to let you pay him in this manner for his equity." You go with Mr. Thomas to talk with the owner of the new home he is buying, and assist him in talking the other owner into accepting monthly payments for his equity with a no cash down payment.

The other seller is happy, Mr. Thomas is happy, and you are happy!

26   Refuse To Negotiate

Here is a technique of negotiating without actually seeming to negotiate. I have found it highly effective in my dealings with sellers.

Sometimes I take the stance: "I don't negotiate." If anyone did this in a rude way, he might be thrown out of the house on his ear!

Of course you have to negotiate. From the time you walk into that seller's house, you are in the act of negotiating. But, I have found that sometimes the most effective technique of negotiating is to appear to be doing the opposite.

In other words, I negotiate by not negotiating. Here's how it works: I walk into a person's house and start chatting with him about his property. Finally, I say, "How much would you like for your home?"

I don't win them all this way, but I win enough. If I want to win more, all I have to do is go out and look at more houses, and get enough "best shots" that I can really handle, at prices low enough that I can buy them comfortably and resell them at a high enough profit to pay me for my time and effort—*it works*!

High Tension Time Limit Technique 27

Here's a technique which is just about the exact opposite of the *tension reduction technique*. I call this technique the *high tension time limit technique.*

Here is the way it works: I go into a house and start talking with the seller, and let him know that buying and reselling houses is my business. This is something you should do. Let the buyer know that you are part of a professional "Mom and Pop" organization. If the seller thinks you represent some big real estate investment company, and your business card confirms that, how do you look to the seller?

That seller is going to think he can get anything out of you. You represent a big real estate investment company, and you have the money! Whatever you do, don't let him think you represent a big investment company. That will drive the price way up.

On the other hand, you don't want to appear too tacky in the eyes of the seller, either. If you look too tacky, then you don't look professional enough. Come across to the seller as a professional, but don't come on as a big shot investor.

I say to the seller, "Now, Mr. Adams, buying and reselling houses is my business. I need to buy two houses before I go home today. This is how I support my family. I have another appointment at 11:45 today, so I will need to leave here in time to make that other appointment".

Then I say, "As I said, before I go home today I need to buy two houses. I hope yours can be one of them. This means we have 45 minutes (I always look at my watch when I'm saying this) to lock everything down if I'm going to buy your home." I let the seller know that I'm very serious about my time. I let him know that this is my business.

I don't use this technique all the time. As I mentioned before, this is almost the exact opposite of the *tension reduction technique.* Obviously, I am putting the seller under a lot of tension now. I am letting him know we only have 45 minutes to negotiate a deal on his house. I keep looking at my watch. I say, "Well, Mr. Adams, we've only got 10 minutes left, and we haven't established an interest rate or the final down payment."

In that initial 45 minutes, I can find out the payments, and everything else I want to know.

Here is the stumbling block. Quite often, people simply don't know anything about their houses in regard to the financial situation. They don't know what their loan balances are, and they don't know what their equity is. Sometimes they don't even know what the monthly payments are on their houses!

You have to ask them if they will pull out the documents so that you can have a look at them yourself. This is very important.

You might see that they bought it three years ago, at a price of $50,000. And now they want to sell it to you for $85,000.

At this point, you say, "Mr. Adams, would you be happy with a 10% increase in your property per year?"

He looks at you and says, "Yes, 10% would be plenty."

You pull out your hand pocket calculator and multiply $50,000 times 1.1, the result of that by 1.1, and the result of that by 1.1 again. While you are doing this, you say, "A 10% increase per year can be calculated by multiplying the house price times 1.1, then multiply that result by 1.1 for the second year, and multiply again by 1.1 for the third year."

Then you show him the final result. "You see, Mr. Adams, if you bought the house for $50,000 three years ago, and it has increased in value 10% per year over these three years, it would be worth $66,550 now."

They see that $80,000 is too much! I give people a time limit in the beginning, and then ask to see those documents. They know we have only a short period of time to negotiate, so they bring everything out quickly, allowing us to get right down to business, and we're able to make a fair deal for both of us that we're happy with. Then, I thank him for his time after signing the documents and go on to the next house I want to buy.

Section 4

Getting Them The Money

Getting Them
The Money

Sometimes, there are properties that are so hot that what you really want to do is give the seller all the cash up front that he wants. But, what if you don't have that kind of cash? After all, you're trying to put as little cash into this property as you can.

You can remedy this in different ways. With a cooperative seller who has a VA or FHA loan, he can get his cash if he gets another VA or FHA loan, and turn the mortgage over to you to pay off. This way, he still gets his cash, and you still get the house, plus a terrific interest rate from his loans you assumed. I have a couple of examples of these types of loan assumptions in this section.

Other good deals on loan assumptions may not be VA or FHA assumable but rather happen to be a loan with a lower than current market interest rate. Hopefully, *all* of the assumable loans will have low interest rates. These are best for you. Since this is not always the case, be prepared to have a little bit of cash on hand in case you need to pay a small down payment in order to get a terrific deal.

VA And FHA Loans   28

One day, in your search for houses, you come across a nice house with a fair market value of $60,000. As you talk with the owner you say, "What is the best price you can give me on your house, Mr. Larsen?"

"$58,000," The seller replies.

You ask, "How much of that is your own equity?"

"$21,500," He looks at you firmly. "And, that's how much cash I want at closing. Then you can assume my loan and start making payments on it to the bank."

"Will you take monthly payments on your equity?"

"No, I've got to have all cash." You request to see his mortgage from the bank. As you look at it, you realize that this is a VA loan, a loan sponsored by the Veteran's Administration. This sheds a whole new light on the situation.

A VA loan is so good that you will consider taking the VA loan instead of trying to talk the seller into taking monthly payments on his equity.

This is the way the VA loan works: the Veteran's Administration does not actually make loans itself, but it does guarantee loans made by banks and other mortgage companies. These loans are available only to veterans. But all of these loans are assumable for any new buyer to purchase the home from the veteran. The new buyer does not have to be a veteran in order to assume this loan!

No down payment is required by the Veteran's Administration. But the buyer is always required to live in the house he is buying under one of these loans.

Also, a qualified veteran can obtain up to 100% financing under one of these loans. The interest rate is lower than regular market interest rates.

One more vital point: the new buyer can buy the home from the veteran without having to qualify for the loan!

You are aware that these loans always have less than market interest rates, and you look eagerly for the line which shows you how much interest is being charged on this particular loan. You find it. The interest rate on this loan is 9%!

You put down the loan document and look up at the seller. "Mr. Larsen, are you a veteran? Are you the one who qualified for this loan in the first place?" He is!

This is what you had been hoping for. You present your offer. "I'll give you $58,000 for your house. And, I'll give you all your equity in cash. But, in order for me to do this, you will have to do one thing for me."

Mr. Larsen looks at you expectantly. "What's that?" he asks.

"Go back to the bank and refinance your house, 10% if possible, on another one of these VA loans. You could qualify for it, I can't. Then, when that loan comes through, you are going to have your $21,500 equity in cold cash, right in your hands. At this point, I come along, buy the house from you, and just assume your two VA mortgage loans with the bank. I'll be making all the monthly payments to the bank, I'll own the house, and you will have your $21,500."

The seller shakes your hand very enthusiastically. "You've got yourself a deal, Mr. Taylor."

In this next example, you are looking through the newspaper, looking for good deals on houses and you come across an ad which says: HOME FOR SALE BY OWNER—ASSUMABLE FHA LOAN.

You don't have to read any further except to get the telephone number off the ad. You make arrangements to meet the owner later in the morning.

You find the house. The home, neighborhood, and landscaping around the property is just fine. It will do either as a rental or as a resale.

You meet the owner and accompany him as he gives you a guided tour of the property. You mention the ad and that the home carried an FHA loan.

"That's right," says Mr. Clark.

"May I take a look at your loan documents on the house?"

He looks a little surprised. "Of course." You go through them and see that this FHA loan is for $44,000. The interest rate is $9^{1}/_{4}\%$. This is much lower than the existing market interest rates.

You will cheerfully assume this loan!

You know you can assume this loan, because you know something about older FHA loans. These loans are insured by the Federal Housing Administration, known as HUD. Again, the older loans are actually made by banks and other regular mortgage companies, but the loans are insured by the FHA, or HUD, and all these loans are fully assumable by a new buyer.

You do not have to live in the house yourself in order to qualify for one of these FHA loans. However, if you do not intend to live in the house yourself, the maximum amount you can finance with one of these loans is about 80% of the purchase price, or 80% of the appraised value, whichever amount is lower.

Since you do not intend to occupy the house yourself, but either rent it or resell it, your best bet is still to get the present owner to qualify for a refinancing loan, since he is actually living in the house, until such time as he sells it.

So you turn to the owner and say, "All right, Mr. Clark, you have a mortgage here for $44,000 on your house. You are selling it at a decent price, at $62,000. I know that's a good fair market value for this home. I am willing to buy your house at that price. You have an equity here of $18,000. Tell me how much of that equity would you like in cash?"

The seller's face registers startled pleasure. "Why, as much of it as I could get."

"Then let's do this. You already qualified for your FHA loan on this house. What I would like you to do now, is to go back and qualify for another FHA loan to refinance this property."

Mr. Clark looks at you with a puzzled expression. "Why do you want me to qualify for the loan? Why don't you go get that loan yourself?"

"Because, I don't intend to live in this house. I intend to rent it out for a while and maybe resell it a little later on. So I could only qualify for 80% of the value of the house, because I would not be living in it. But you are living in it, so you could qualify for as much as 95% of the home's value. Do you see what I mean?"

You take out your pocket calculator. "You're asking $62,000 for the house? Was the house appraised at that value?"

The seller nods. "Yes, I set the price at exactly the appraised value."

"All right then," you work with the calculator. "Ninety-five percent of $62,000 is $58,900. Your mortgage is $44,000. Subtract that $44,000 from $58,900, and you get $14,900. This means that if they let you borrow up to the full 95% of the appraised value, you'll end up with $14,900 cash. Then, I will come in and buy the house from you, and assume both your loans. I won't give you any down payment, but you'll have $14,900 cash from that second loan. But I'll have the house and I'll be making payments on the loans, and you'll have the $14,900 cash for your equity."

"You have a total equity in this house of $18,000. That's $62,000 minus your $44,000 first mortgage. If you borrow the $14,900 on the second loan, then that will leave you $3,100 in equity that I have not paid you for yet. I'll just give you a mortgage note on that and make you regular monthly payments until it's paid off."

"I'll pay you $31 a month; that's 1% per month." You are writing all these figures down on a paper and showing them to the seller. "What about it, Mr. Clark? Do you think this is a fair deal I'm offering you? You'll be able to walk away from your transaction with up to $14,900 in your pocket."

Mr. Clark seems a little stunned by all this. He finally says, "Yes, I'll have the money in cash."

One hour at his bank, and Mr. Clark ends up with a briefcase full of cash, you end up with a house with no cash down payment, and you are both very happy!

Conventional Loan: Second Mortgage Crank   29

You have been diligently passing out your cards all over town, publicizing the fact that you are interested in buying houses. You talk to friends, chance acquaintances, and anyone else you meet. You are getting your name out there as a real estate investor.

One morning, you received a call from an Arnold Wilkinson. He tells you he is putting his home up for sale. "I haven't advertised it yet, and when this friend of mine told me about you, I thought I would contact you first. Would you be interested in buying my house? If we could come to an agreement, I wouldn't even put the advertisement in the paper. I would just go ahead and sell it to you."

"I'm always interested in buying houses. If the price is right, and the terms are favorable, we can go ahead and complete a transaction today."

You go out to see the house. It is a decent looking house in a respectable suburban neighborhood. The owner meets you at the door and shows you through the house. As always, you look around carefully. You run through your checklist, and everything indicates that the house is in good shape.

"How much are you asking for your house, Mr. Wilkinson?"

"$72,000. I had it appraised last month, and that was the value the appraiser placed on it."

"Yes," you say, "that seems a fair price for it. May I see the appraisal papers, and while I'm looking at that, may I have a look at your mortgage papers, also? I need to get all the information I can about the house and the financing."

The seller nods. "That's understandable. Please have a chair while I get the documents."

Presently, Mr. Wilkinson returns and places both the appraisal papers and mortgage papers on the table. You scan through them.

The appraisal is a professional job. This house obviously has a fair market value of $72,000. The mortgage papers indicate that the balance of the mortgage is now at $46,000. The interest rate is $11^1/_2$%.

"I know your house appraised at $72,000. Would you sell it to me for something less than that if I could give you a sizable cash down payment?"

"I might consider that, Mr. Taylor. How much cash would you be willing to pay me?"

"You would have $10,000 cash at the closing. I could afford to do this if you would be willing to come down enough on the price of the house. What would be the lowest price you could sell the house for, and still be comfortable with? If I could handle that price, I'd buy your house, and arrange for your $10,000 cash."

"I can sell you the house at a price of $67,000, if I get the $10,000 in cash at the closing."

"Fine," you say. "Now, this is the way I can get you your $10,000. You go down to the bank and take out a second mortgage on your home, a second mortgage for $10,000."

"That will be your $10,000 cash. When we close our transaction and I buy your house, I will assume both of your loans, the first mortgage and the second mortgage. By the way, make sure that the second mortgage will be completely assumable by me. When I buy the house from you, I want to be able to assume both of your loans. The first mortgage is for $46,000, and the second mortgage will be for $10,000. Those add up to $56,000. Since I am buying the house from you at a price of $67,000, I will still owe you $11,000 for your equity which you will still have in the house. I'll give you a third mortgage and an $11,000 note for your equity."

Mr. Wilkinson has been following all this with intense interest. "I see how that would work, Mr. Taylor. I'll agree to go ahead with our transaction on these terms."

The seller's loan was neither VA or FHA, but his existing first mortgage was at an interest rate of 11½%, still much lower than the new mortgage rates. Of course, after he agrees to get the second mortgage, you will want to see if he can possibly qualify for a VA or FHA loan on the second mortgage. Always try for the VA loan first, that is the best. Then try for the FHA loan. This is second best. If the buyer cannot qualify for either of these, then go ahead with a second mortgage on a conventional loan. In this case, the seller cannot qualify for either the VA or FHA loan, so you go ahead with the conventional loan. But, you do not want to refinance all the cash you can on this second mortgage because the interest rate will be too high. In this case, just use the second mortgage crank to get enough payment coming from the second mortgage, not from you!

You then give the seller a third mortgage on the rest of his equity, paying him a much lower interest rate than the bank will be charging for the conventional second mortgage. Try for 9% or 10% interest on the loan from the seller himself.

30 Conventional Mortgage: First Mortgage Crank

You have placed an ad in the newspaper which reads: "Real estate investor interested in buying houses." Your phone number is included at the end of the ad. Your telephone rings. "Hello, Mr. Taylor. Are you the real estate investor mentioned in the newspaper ad?"

"Yes, I am. Do you have a house for sale?"

"Yes," she says. "Might you be interested in buying it?"

"Yes, I'm always interested, if the price and the terms are right. When may I see the house?"

"Any time this afternoon," she replies. "My name is Mrs. Burke. The house is on 1139 Hiawatha Drive."

When you arrive, you are impressed. The home is older but sturdily built. The landscaping is immaculate and the property boasts a number of large shade trees. The neighborhood is peaceful and quiet. You know there will be no trouble either renting or reselling this property.

Introductions concluded, she shows you through the house. Everything has a look of order and cleanliness about it.

You ask why she is selling the house. She looks a little sad. "It is a very nice house, Mr. Taylor. I hate to leave it, but my husband died a few months ago, and my daughter and her family have invited me to come and live with them in Southern California. At this stage in my life, I really think that this is the thing for me to do."

"I would do exactly the same thing under those circumstances, Mrs. Burke. I want you to know that I will buy your house if I can afford the price and the terms. It is really a lovely home. What would be the lowest price you could accept for it, and still feel right about it? I wouldn't want to cheat you."

"That's kind of you, Mr. Taylor. The man from the bank, the one who does appraisals for mortgages, said that $55,000 would be a fair price for the house. But, I don't really need that much for it. I would be content with $50,000."

"That's very reasonable of you. May I look at your mortgage papers? I assume you do have a mortgage on the place."

"Yes, I do. I pulled them out of the drawer when I knew you were coming. Here they are on the desk."

After digesting the papers she had given you, you see she has a balance of only $9,500 on her existing mortgage. Her equity is $40,500. You ask if she would be willing to allow you to pay her equity in monthly payments. She agrees, but says she would need some cash in the beginning. Her daughter's family has had some expenses lately and she wants to help out. She feels $5,000 would meet her requirements.

You notice that the interest rate on the existing mortgage is 13$\frac{1}{2}$%. This is the same interest rate that the banks are charging now for new mortgages. You would gain nothing by using the second mortgage crank to get Mrs. Burke the money.

This is a perfect situation for a first mortgage crank. You will want to borrow just enough money to give Mrs. Burke her $5,000 cash down payment. You do not want to borrow any more than necessary because the interest rate is too high. You know you can get a lower interest by giving Mrs. Burke a second mortgage on her remaining equity in the property.

Always have the owner take out the new loan whenever possible. The bank knows this individual and is less likely to give them problems.

Take out a new first mortgage for enough money to repay the old first mortgage and give Mrs. Burke her $5,000. Make sure that you will be able to assume the loan after she takes it out, and that all new buyers in the future will also have the right to assume that loan. Then you buy her house and assume her loan from the bank, her first mortgage. You give her the $5,000 cash as a down payment and give her a second mortgage on the rest of her equity, which will be (you work this out on your pocket calculator in front of her, so she can see what you are doing) the $50,000 sale price of the house minus the $9,500 existing first mortgage, minus the $5,000 for your down payment, leaving her with an equity of $33,500. You'll give her a second mortgage on her equity, and make her monthly payments of 1% per month on that $35,500 until the whole thing is paid off. Your monthly payments to her will be $355. You'll pay her an interest rate of 9% on that second mortgage.

You remind her that those monthly payments will be coming in for many years and eventually will become part of her estate. Her daughter and her family will always have something to remember her by.

Of course, you make sure that Mrs. Burke is not able to qualify for a VA loan or an FHA loan. Only then do you go ahead with the conventional loan. In this case, the conventional loan will work well, because you only need to borrow a small amount. Even though the interest rate is high, the total principle of the loan is relatively small, so you will not be paying too much interest.

Section 5

The
Buyer
Gets
A Loan

The Buyer
Gets A Loan

There are times when a seller is unable or unwilling to sell his property without receiving a sizable cash down payment. If you do not have the cash required for the down payment, you have two options: 1) either you do not buy the property, or 2) you borrow the money you need.

Banks are in business to lend people money. You can always approach a bank and request a loan for the money needed for the seller's down payment. Sometimes your request will be denied, and sometimes you will receive the money you need.

Going to a bank is not my favorite way of borrowing money. I prefer to turn the seller into a bank, but this does not always work. When I do find a bank that is cooperative with me, I like to get to know the people so they remember me the next time I need their help getting loans.

Usually, when you go into a bank for a loan the bank officer asks for collateral on the loan. If you own your home already, it is a good source for collateral for a loan, and the bank officer could offer you a loan for about 80 to 90% of the value of your home.

On the other hand, if you don't own a home, where do you go for venture capital? Is your car worth very much? Do you have credit cards? Think of ways you can use your car for collateral if it has value, or put the charge on your credit cards after figuring out how much you are allowed to borrow on them. I'll show you an example of one particular scenario in this section along with other ways where you, as the buyer, can get a loan or other ways to help with the purchase of a property. By the way, some of these ideas are very clever!

Bank Loans For Down Payments

31

In this deal, the owner has a $30,000 mortgage which you can assume, and he is willing to take monthly payments on his equity, at 10% interest. So far, everything looks good about this deal.

There is just one catch. The owner simply must have $4,000 as a cash down payment. Unfortunately, you do not have $4,000 in cash!

You walk into the bank and explain the situation to the loan officer. "Mr. Sims, I found this nice home I can buy for $48,000. The owner is Ed Johnson, who has his mortgage on the house right here with your bank."

"Oh, yes," says Mr. Sims. "I am familiar with the mortgage."

"Mr. Johnson has agreed to sell his house to me and let me assume his mortgage. I want to be sure I can assume it from him when I buy the house."

"Just a minute, Mr. Taylor. I will go pull the mortgage from the file and we'll have a look at it." He gets the mortgage from the file and the two of you look at it together.

"Yes," he says. "You can assume it."

"There's one more thing I've got to know. Will I be able to assume that loan at the same rate of interest? He has 10½% interest on the mortgage."

"Yes, you will."

"All right," you say. "If I can get a statement from you in writing to that effect, then I'll be able to assume the loan when I buy the property."

"That can be arranged. I'll have the secretary type up a statement to that effect."

While she is typing the agreement, Mr. Sims says, "I can see you've had some experience in real estate dealings. Have you had a bad experience with some banks in the past?"

"Frankly, yes. Actually, a friend of mine had the experience. He was buying a piece of property and wanted to assume the owner's loan. The loan officer at the bank, not your bank, assured him that he could assume that loan with the same monthly payments and at the same interest rate. When he bought the house about a month later, the bank let him assume the loan but at a higher interest rate and at a higher monthly payment!"

"I just want to make doubly sure that something like that never happens to me."

"I don't blame you a bit," says Mr. Sims.

"I need to talk with you about something else, too. Mr. Johnson will sell me his house and let me assume his mortgage, and he will let me give him a second mortgage for the rest of his equity. I'll be making him monthly payments on it, but he needs $4,000 down in cash. I don't have $4,000 right now. Could you lend me the $4,000 for the down payment?"

Mr. Sims shakes his head. "I'm sorry, but the bank couldn't do that. This would mean that you would be buying the house with 100% financing. That would be a poor business practice for the bank, and I know the underwriter would never approve it. If you haven't actually bought into any equity in the house, except with money you've borrowed from us to buy the equity, then you don't really have any equity in that property. Only this bank and Mr. Johnson would actually own equity in that house. So the bank would not be able to approve a loan to provide cash for you to make a down payment on the house. Do you see the logic in this?"

"Yes, I see the logic in it," you say. You have been down this road before, and you know where it leads, so you might as well get there as quickly as possible.

"I do have a building lot over on 7th West. I have $7,000 worth of equity in that. Would you lend me $4,000 on that building lot?"

Mr. Sims brightens. "Certainly. There should be no problem."

"All right, then, I'll go ahead and borrow the $4,000 on the building lot and use that as the cash down payment on Mr. Johnson's house."

"That will be fine," says Mr. Sims. "You will actually own $4,000 worth of equity in the Johnson house, and the bank will consider you a good risk."

If this bank had not loaned you the $4,000 on your building lot, you would simply have gone to another bank and borrowed the $4,000. Then, you would pay that money to Mr. Johnson for his down payment, and the seller's bank would neither know nor care where you raised that $4,000 cash.

Home Equity Loans 32

People often overlook a potential source of funds for financing any business venture they would care to undertake. This source of money lies right under their feet—and also over their heads—their own homes!

Let's look at an example here. Jean Parker is an intelligent, young woman, ambitious and yearning for success. She is happily married and has two fine children. Both are in school, so she has extra time on her hands. She would like to help her husband provide for their family. They own their own home in a lovely suburban neighborhood.

Jean decided on real estate as a money making venture. She knows other women who have succeeded in real estate investment with less intelligence and education than herself.

She thinks, "If they can do it, I can do it!" She set out to try. She hears through the neighborhood grapevine that one of the neighbors four blocks away is moving to Chicago. This looks like her golden opportunity.

That afternoon, she goes to the Watson home and rings the doorbell. Mrs. Watson, a middle-aged lady, opens the door. She enters the house where Mrs. Watson ushers her to an easy chair. After they chat for a few minutes, Jean says, "Well, Mrs. Watson, I hear you're leaving us."

"Yes, Clarence has been transferred to Chicago. We'll be moving there soon. We still have some things to take care of here first, though, like selling the house and a few other things."

"You do have a lovely home. Have you put it up for sale yet?"

"No, not yet. We had an appraiser come and look at the house, and he said it's worth $54,000. We haven't decided what real estate broker to go with, if we do go with a broker. We might just advertise it ourselves."

Jean takes a deep breath and gathers her courage.

"Mrs. Watson, I would be interested in buying your house."

Mrs. Watson looks surprised. "Oh really! Well . . . this is a surprise."

"May I see the house?"

"Of course. Come along, and I'll show you through." The house has no serious defects, and Jean determines to buy it. "I really would like to buy your house Mrs. Watson. Would you let it go for $51,000? I think that's about all we could afford right now."

"Oh, I surely think so. Of course, I'll have to speak with Clarence when he comes home from work this evening, but I think that price would be all right."

Jean goes back that evening to speak with both Mr. and Mrs. Watson. They receive her cordially. "Well, Mrs. Parker, I hear that you are interested in buying our house."

"Yes, I think we can afford to buy it if you will sell it for about $51,000."

"We've been talking it over, and decided that we will accept that offer and sell the house to you."

Jean is flushed with success. "Wonderful!"

"Of course," Mr. Watson adds, "We'll really need to have some cash as a down payment on our equity. About $4,000 should do it."

"Yes, we would. We'll take back a second mortgage from you and you can send your monthly payments to us in Chicago."

Jean leaves the Watson home trying to think of a way of coming up with the $4,000 cash down payment.

The following day she walks into her bank to speak with the loan officer. "Mr. Sanford, I'm going into real estate investing and I need $4,000 for a down payment on a lovely home I've found. Could you arrange a loan for me?"

Mr. Sanford smiles. "We should be able to arrange that. What would you put up for collateral?"

"Collateral?" Jean thinks rapidly. Collateral, what in the world do we have that we could use for collateral?

"We have to have some kind of collateral," explains Mr. Sanford. "Do you own anything that's worth $4,000?"

"No, not a thing. Except—our house! How could I have forgotten our house?" Mr. Sanford chuckles. "People are always doing that. They forget all about their houses as collateral. I guess that's because they are living inside the houses, and see them every day, and they just take them for granted. But they're just about the best source of collateral when you're looking for a loan."

"How much could we borrow on our house?" asks Jean.

"We could lend you up to 80% of the value of your home. Of course, your first mortgage would be figured in as part of that 80%."

"How much would the interest rate be?"

"We just charge the prime rate plus 2%. The prime rate is 11% right now, so we would charge you 13% interest."

"Wonderful!" exclaims Jean. "All I need to borrow is $4,000, but it's nice to know that the equity in our home is there, whenever we need to borrow money on it."

33   Credit Cards

Credit cards are another forgotten source of funds for venture capital. Let's look at an example:

John Horton has found a really good buy in a single family dwelling in a nice section of town. The price is $58,500, with an existing mortgage of $34,500. This gives the owner an equity of $24,000.

He negotiates with the owner. "Mr. Caldwell, would you consider accepting monthly payments from me on your $24,000 equity? I would give you a second mortgage on it and pay you 1%, or $240 a month."

"Well," Mr. Caldwell considers, "I couldn't take it all in monthly payments. I've got to have some cash up front."

"How much do you really need right now?" John Horton asks.

Mr. Caldwell calculates in his head. "I would say that $4,500 ought to do it."

"Done. I'll get that money for you one way or another."

He walks out of the house and begins to think. How can he raise $4,500 quick enough to make this deal? He knows that he has to come through with the money immediately, or Mr. Caldwell will sell the house right out from under him. He can't afford to spend too much time trying to raise this money.

What could he do? He owns no home. He has no real estate anywhere yet; he is only beginning as a real estate investor. He does own a car, but it is not worth more than $1,500 at the most. He has to do something really creative to come up with this $4,500 right now.

He climbs into his car and drives down the street. He pulls into the gas station on the corner and drives up to the self-serve pump. He fills his tank and walks over to the cashier's window. "That will be $18.72, please. Will that be cash or charge?" John pulls out his billfold. He has only $14.00 cash. "I guess it will have to be charge today." He pulls out his Master Card and hands it over to the young lady.

She accepts the card and says, "Do you have any other form of identification? A driver's license, a credit card?"

He shows her his driver's license and his Visa card. She completes the transaction with the Master Card and hands it back to him.

"Thank you," he says, putting the charge cards back into his billfold, next to his First Security charge card.

He stares for a moment at all these credit cards. "*Eureka!*" he exclaims. John Horton looks at each one of his credit cards, calculating the amount he is allowed to borrow on each one. He realizes that by borrowing on these credit cards separately, he can borrow the $4,500 he needs to purchase Mr. Caldwell's home.

34   NOW Accounts

Mary Soloman decides to enter the field of real estate investing. She is young, single, attractive, and has big plans for her life. She has no desire at all to become a starving artist.

She has a part-time job as a teller in the First Security Bank. Her hours fluctuate, and she spends all her free time working on her art.

She would like to become wealthy enough to support herself while she pursues her art career.

She has decided that real estate investment is her means to that end. She is in no position to quit her job at the bank just yet, and knows she will have to get her real estate business going first.

She begins by doing all the things she knows she should do to get into the real estate investment business. She tells all her friends that she is interested in buying real estate, watches ads in the newspaper every day, and has contacted a real estate broker in her part of town.

One afternoon after work, she spots an ad in the newspaper which looks promising. It reads: STARTER HOME, LOW DOWN, GOOD TERMS. She calls the phone number in the ad and agrees to meet the owner of the property in a half hour. Mary drives out to see the place, and it looks good. If she were married and starting a family, this would be an ideal place for her to live. She parks the car, walks up to the house, and rings the doorbell.

A young man answers the door. "Hello there. Mary Soloman, I presume?"

"That's right, and you must be Fred Burgener."

"The same. Won't you come in and see the house?" Mary walks into the house and Fred proceeds to give her the grand tour, showing her everything from the basement to the attic. She spends quite a bit of time in the kitchen which has, among other things, a built-in oven and dishwasher.

"Well," she says, "this looks like a homey little house. How much are you asking for it?"

"$45,000," says Fred.

"That sounds reasonable. I don't know whether I could quite afford it at that price, though."

Fred looks disappointed. "How much could you afford?"

"Actually, I can only afford about $42,000 right now."

Fred looks at Mary, thinking it over. Finally he says, "I guess that would be enough."

"Do you have a mortgage on the house?"

"Yes, it's for $28,500."

"Then if you sell the house to me at $42,000, you have an equity there of $13,500. May I make regular monthly payments to you on that equity? I'll give you 10% interest on the principle, and pay you off at 1% per month. That will give you payments of $135 a month. Of course, I'll give you a second mortgage to secure the loan."

Fred looks at her again, really thinking it over. "Maybe . . . but . . . I must have $2,200 down."

"The sounds okay to me," Mary replies. "I'll have the money for you by the time we close the sale."

Mary walks out of the house in a mixed state of euphoria and bafflement. $2,200! "Where in the world am I going to get $2,200 in cash?!"

She is still thinking about it the next morning at work. She sees all this money coming across the window to her, and can't stop thinking about the $2,200 she needs to buy this house.

As she goes into the bookkeeping section, she overhears a customer telling one of the bookkeepers, "No, we won't charge him an overdraft charge. He has a NOW account. That gives him overdraft protection up to $2,500."

Mary stands there staring at her for a moment. The NOW account!

"Excuse me," she says, "May I ask you a question?"

"Of course, what is it?"

"It's about this NOW account. You can write a check for up to $2,500 over the amount you actually have in your checking account, but then what happens?" The customer replies, "Then you can either pay it all back when you see that you are short on funds in your account, or you can arrange to pay it back in small monthly payments."

Mary sighs, "Ahhh . . . Thank you very much." Mary Soloman has just successfully joined the ranks of the real estate investors. Good luck to you Mary, on your art career!

Buy Low,
Refinance High

35

Bill Wellman is a very successful real estate investor. This is evident by the huge amount of cash reserves he has in his checking, savings, and certificates of deposit.

He also owns a great deal of real estate. He has publicized his status as a real estate investor by advertising in newspapers, handing out cards, and in general, just making himself as famous as possible. Brokers and private parties come to him when they have good deals to offer in real estate buys. He is a firm believer in buying real estate with little or no cash down; this is the way he has made his fortune in real estate investment.

Bright and early one morning, his telephone rings. He answers it. "Hello, Bill Wellman speaking."

"Hello, Mr. Wellman," comes a rather distraught-sounding man's voice. "This is Arthur Destrata. I know that you're a real estate investor, and I want to show you some real estate I have for sale. When would be the soonest you could come and look at it?"

Bill Wellman hears the urgency in the other man's voice, and knows that this has the look of a good real estate deal. This man sounds like a highly-motivated seller. "Oh, perhaps I could drop by sometime this morning."

"I'll be waiting for you," says the caller. "The address is 1179 Cholla Lane."

Bill strolls leisurely up to the house looking the place over. It has seen better days. He can see that the roof needs some repair, the house is broken in spots, and the front yard has gone to weeds. But, the house itself seems solid, and with some fixing up, it could still be a good deal, depending, of course, on the price he would have to pay to purchase it.

He meets the owner and the pair tour the house together. Bill sees that the inner walls can use some touching up here and there, and the ceiling in one of the bedrooms needs to be re-done.

"How much are you asking for the place, Mr. Destrata?"

"I would take $28,000 for it." He looks at Bill urgently. "But I've got to have cash, all cash."

Bill considers his answer. He has made his fortune in real estate by buying with little or no cash down. The very idea of shelling out $28,000 of his precious cash for this miserable hovel absolutely appalls him.

He shakes his head slowly. "I'm afraid that's out of the question, Mr. Destrata. If I bought this place at all, I would buy it with little, if any, cash down." The seller looks even more desperate. "I'll sell it to you for $26,000 then, if I can just get cash for it! I'm willing to make a real sacrifice here, if you'll give me all cash."

Bill Wellman looks the place over carefully. He has bought "fixer-uppers" before, and he can estimate the cost of fixing the property up so that it will sell at a fair market value. He looks around and estimates that it will cost about $3,500 to repair and that it would resell at a fair market value of $37,000, possibly $40,000. He says to Mr. Destrata, "I estimate that it would take about $3,500 to fix this place up right. Would you be willing to put out that much money to renovate this property?"

"Yes," replies Mr. Destrata anxiously, "If I had the time and the money to do it!"

"Then would you be willing to lower the price another $3,500 so that I would have that much to work with in renovating the place?"

"Yes," Mr. Destrata assures him.

"All right, then," Bill Wellman says. "I will give you $23,500 for the place, all in cash."

"It's a deal, Mr. Wellman."

Bill Wellman buys the house for cash at a price of $23,500, quickly renovates it at a cost of $3,100, and then goes to a bank to refinance the house. He was able to assume the existing first mortgage of $12,000 on the house, so his cash outlay was really only $11,500. Now he wants to refinance it for as much as he can on a second mortgage. This will allow him to get back as much cash as possible on the property. The bank sends an appraiser out. He appraises the house at $39,500. The bank will loan up to 80% of the appraised value of the house, which is $31,600. He already has the underlying first mortgage of $12,000, so his loan on the second mortgage ends up $19,600.

After the dust has cleared, Bill Wellman has actually paid out, above the $12,000 first mortgage, $13,500 of his own cash for the house. When he refinanced the house, the bank gave him a loan of $19,600 on the second mortgage.

This leaves Bill Wellman with $6,100 more cash than in the beginning. He ended up buying this house with no cash down and over $6,000 cash back!

Combination: Small Down Payment Plus Graduated Monthly Payments

36

Dave Spencer has been buying and selling real estate for some time now. He has made many different offers to many different sellers. Some of these offers have been accepted. Others have not.

He has learned to combine his techniques, and finds that most of the time his offers end up as a combination of more than one technique.

Here is an example: Dave finds a home in the suburbs. He has called the owner on the phone and the owner is expecting him that afternoon.

He finds the owner, Mr. Lou Flint, a congenial, laid-back type, who seems to have no great sense of urgency in selling his property right away. Dave decides that this man is not a highly-motivated seller.

However, he is a seller. Dave goes through the house with him, looking everything over. Everything looks good. Mr. Flint brings out a professional appraisal; the house is appraised at $63,000. He shows Dave the mortgage papers. The home has a mortgage of $50,000 on it.

"You have an equity of $13,000," says Dave. "Will you take monthly payments from me on that equity? I'll give you a $13,000 note with a second mortgage on the house."

The seller thinks it over, and finally decides that yes, he is willing to accept monthly payments for his equity. "But if I take monthly payments on my equity, I'm going to want $6,000 cash down."

This is just under 10% of the purchase price, and this sounds good to Dave. Still, he makes a counter offer. "How about $3,000 down? Then you'll have $10,000 equity left, and I'll give you a $10,000 mortgage for that equity and pay you in monthly payments."

Dave generally offers 1% per month on the monthly payment. If this payment were on the entire $13,000, it would be $530 per month. He is not concerned about the length of time required to pay off his loan. His basic concern is the affordability of this property. The 1% per month repayment schedule is just a good target for him to shoot at.

In this case, 1% per month on the $10,000 mortgage would be $100 per month. But in this case, he cannot afford to pay the $100 a month right in the beginning. So he makes this offer: "Mr. Flint, I'll be taking over your first mortgage and making monthly payments of $520 to the bank. I intend to rent this property for a while. Hopefully, I can rent it for about $540 per month. That's $20 a month more than I will be paying on the first mortgage. Therefore, I'd like to give you that $3,000 in cash you want as a down payment. In return, I would like for you to let me pay you at a rate of $20 per month for the first year. The second year that will increase $20 for seven years. After that, I'll be paying you $160 per month, and I'll continue that $160 per month for the remainder of the loan."

Lou Flint thinks this one over. "Yes, I'd be willing to settle for payments like that, as long as I get my initial $3,000 in cash."

If Dave Spencer had made monthly payments of $100 a month in the beginning on that $10,000 second mortgage, at 1% per month of the $10,000 total, his monthly payments would have been $520 for the first mortgage, plus, his $100 a month on the second mortgage, the total being $620 a month. Since he can only rent the property for $540 a month, this means he would have lost $80 every month on the deficit between his property payments and his income from the rental. Assuming rents go up at 5% per year, then every year he will be able to add $25 extra to that monthly rent. Every year he is adding $20 a month to his monthly property payment to Mr. Flint. This means every year he is gaining an increase of $5 per month on his net income. ($25 increase in rental income minus $20 per month second mortgage payment.) He will, therefore, stay ahead of the game all the way! I want you to know, I never buy properties unless I can get graduated payments on them. Real estate investors who are in this business for keeps are creating long term income. If we do not learn how to get low monthly payments in the beginning, we will be in danger of going out of business. Those investors who are alive, well and happy with their investments are those who have learned how to get low monthly payments so that they can get and keep their property!

37

Establishing
Commercial Credit

Linda Bradley has decided that the best thing for her to do is to go into real estate investment. Her biggest problem is that she has no cash for down payments. She has found several homes which she would liked to purchase, but she always runs into the problem of not having the cash needed for the down payment. Linda has no home of her own or any other real estate property and, as she runs through her inventory of things she owns, there is nothing of value that could possibly be used as collateral for a loan.

She is employed at a large department store and her salary is just enough to make her living expenses and cover her car payment. Her small savings account would only allow her to safely use $500, not nearly enough to get started as a real estate investor.

There must be another way. Then she learns about commercial credit. She discovers that commercial credit can be very valuable for a real estate investor. She talks with a commercial loan officer in the bank and soon realizes that he is very understanding of a real estate investor's needs. He knows they need money up front in their transactions, money for down payments, and money to use in repairing and improving properties they are buying. She learns that she can get loans with far less security, because these loans are what are called short-term loans. When she wants to buy and resell a property quickly, the commercial loan is a very good way to go. But, how is she to establish commercial credit? She thinks seriously about it for a few days, and makes inquiries of other real estate investors. She learns from one of them about a very effective technique for establishing commercial credit.

She does not hesitate to put this plan into action. She already has $500 of her own that she could use for this project. She could withdraw it from her savings account and not run short on her living expenses. But, she still needs an additional $500 for this plan. She approaches her friend Norma, who also works in the store.

"Norma, I have a big favor to ask of you. I would like you to lend me $500. I only need it for about three months."

Norma looks nervous. "What are you going to use it for? If you're going to take that $500 and go out and speculate on a real estate investment . . . "

"No, no, nothing like that," Linda assures her. "I'll keep it all in my savings account, I promise you."

"A savings account? Why do you want to borrow money from me if you are just going to turn around and put it into a savings account?"

Linda explains her entire plan to Norma. "This is something I've got to see. All right, I'll lend you the $500."

Linda borrows the $500 from Norma and then withdraws the $500 from her own personal account. She takes this $1,000, walks into the Bank of America, and starts a savings account.

She then proceeds downstairs to the commercial loan officer's desk. "Mr. Donaldson, I'd like to apply for a commercial loan. I need $1,000, and I'll sign a note to repay at the end of 90 days." "What would you use this money for?" asks Mr. Donaldson.

"I want to use it for business purposes."

"What will you be putting up for collateral, Linda?"

"I have $1,000 in a savings account right here in your bank."

"All right! We'll give you the loan."

Of course they'll give her this loan! They're just lending Linda her own money. They are also going to charge her interest on it. Banks love customers like Linda!

So Linda walks out of the Bank of America with a $1,000 commercial loan, payable in 90 days.

She takes this $1,000 and goes into the Bonneville Bank, depositing the $1,000 in a savings account there. She borrows her $1,000 back again on a commercial loan from the Bonneville Bank.

She deposits this $1,000 in the Commercial Bank and Trust, and borrows it back again on another commercial loan.

She deposits this $1,000 in the Citizen's Bank, and gets another $1,000 commercial loan from this bank. Finally, she takes this $1,000 and deposits it in a savings account in the Wells Fargo Bank, leaving it there to draw interest. She can use this interest to help in paying the interest on the loans from the other four banks.

She has made sure that there is no penalty for early repayment on any of these 90 day loans. At the end of a month or so, Linda withdraws her $1,000 from the Wells Fargo Bank, and uses it to pay off her $1,000 commercial loan from the Bank of America. She has to pay interest on it, but it is only one month's worth because she is paying it off early. She walks right up to Mr. Donaldson, commercial loan officer, and gives him the money. "Here you are, Mr. Donaldson."

Mr. Donaldson is impressed. "You are paying the loan off early. You've only had the money for a month."

Linda smiles at him. "I'm in the real estate business. From time to time I'll be needing ready cash for real estate investment. You'll be seeing me in here again."

"Any time, Miss Bradley. Your credit is good with us." And that's it! Linda has just established commercial credit at her first bank!

She is not through yet, however. Now that she has paid back her loan at the Bank of America, she is able to withdraw her $1,000 from her savings account at the Bank of America and proceed to pay off her commercial loan at the Bonneville Bank. She goes on down the line, paying off each loan and withdrawing her money from her savings account in that particular bank in person. He will remember her next time she wants to get a commercial loan.

Finally, she withdraws her $1,000 from the Citizen's Bank, and gives her friend Norma her $500 back. Norma looks at the money in her hand and says, "Thanks for paying me back so soon. And how did your plan work?"

"Great! I've now got commercial credit at four different banks!"

With a good commercial credit rating at four banks, Linda is all set to borrow money quickly for down payments, repair work on "fixer-uppers," and anything else she needs quick money to do in the real estate field. She will, of course have to pay the interest on these loans, but if she resells the properties quickly, she will be able to pay these loans back before too much interest is due. This interest is small compared to the large profits she will make in real estate investments.

Local Finance Company Loans **38**

Jim Wheeler has just found a fixer-upper. It is not a nice looking house, but it could be if it were fixed up right. He knows that when the needed repairs are completed, the house will have a fair market value of $45,000.

He talks with the owner, "Mr. Webb, what is the lowest price you would take for this property?"

Mr. Webb thinks it over. "I'd sell it for $35,000."

Jim considers. "Sorry, that's a little more than I could pay." He turns and starts to walk toward the door.

"Wait!" calls Mr. Webb. "What price could you afford?"

"The most I could pay for this place, and still have it be a good enough deal that I could buy it, would be $32,000."

"I suppose I could sell the place to you for $32,000, if you'll give me $9,000 cash."

"It's a deal," says Jim. Jim calls in his contractor to find out how much money he will need to fix this place up for resale. The contractor says, "Not more than $2,200. I'll try to do it for less, maybe $2,000."

Jim has to raise a total of $11,500 to buy the property: $9,000 cash for the seller and $2,500 to pay his contractor.

He goes into his bank where he has a small checking account and speaks with the loan officer. "Mr. Overton, I need to borrow $11,500. I'm buying a property, and I need the money to buy out the owner's equity and to fix the place up for resale."

"May I see your purchase contract?" asks Mr. Overton. Jim reaches into his briefcase and pulls out his purchase contract. Mr. Overton studies it carefully. "I'm sorry, Mr. Wheeler, but our bank would never approve such a loan. You aren't really putting any of your own money into this property. If we lend you this money, you'll be buying this property with 100% financing.

Now Jim Wheeler has a real problem. The following day, he sees an ad in the newspaper advertising the Austin Finance Company.

Thirty minutes later, he is in their office, speaking with the loan officer. "Mr. Cartwright, I am buying a property over on the west side, and I would like to borrow $11,500. Will the Austin Finance Company lend me the money?"

"We might," says Mr. Cartwright, "If you have enough equity in the property. We will lend you up to 80% of the appraised value."

Mr. Cartwright does not even ask to see Jim's purchase contract! As long as he can see there is enough equity in the property to cover the amount of the loan, the contract itself is unimportant.

Mr. Cartwright goes out with Jim to appraise the property. He appraises it at $41,000 as is. He can see that it would be worth $45,000 or $46,000 if it were fixed up. "Okay," says Mr. Cartwright. "I can see that you'll have enough equity in the property to cover the loan."

These local finance companies do not care about your purchase contract, or whether you paid any money down on the property. They only want to be sure that you have enough equity in that property to cover that loan they are making.

They do charge high interest rates however, so you should only borrow from these local finance companies when you're buying property for a quick resale and quick profit. You can then pay back that finance company quickly, before the interest eats you up.

Operating Line Of Credit   **39**

Martin Eldred is a part-time real estate investor. He spends most of his time working at his regular job. When he does go out to look for real estate investments, he strives to get the most effective use of his time.

He looks for real estate buys every Saturday, and sometimes evenings during the week. He found a good deal two weeks ago. The seller seemed agreeable to his terms, but did need some cash. He did not have the ready cash, so he went to a bank and applied for a loan. There were delays in the loans approval and when it did come through, he went back to talk to the seller of the house and discovered the seller had received another offer and had accepted it.

Martin realizes that when he finds a good opportunity in real estate, he must get the money together quickly, or he may lose the deal.

He searches for a solution to the problem. He decides to go to the professionals. He goes to his bank, where he has his savings account, and talks with the loan officer. "Mr. Daley, I have a problem here. I'm a real estate investor, and I am going to be making real estate investments regularly. Occasionally, I will need to borrow money for these transactions. I know sometimes it can take a while for a loan to come through, and I would like to know what you would suggest to help me get the money I need quickly."

Mr. Daley leans back in his chair. "They have a word for what you want. Actually, it's a phrase. They call it "An Operating Line of Credit." The first thing we have to do is to check out your credit rating. We have to know how much you are good for. You do have an account with our bank, don't you?"

"Yes. That's why I came here to talk with you."

"All right. It should be fairly easy for us to check out your credit rating. I'll put the wheels in motion right away."

The bank checks out Martin's credit rating and calls him back in. "Mr. Eldred, we checked out your credit rating, and the bank says you're good for up to $14,000 on your signature."

Mr. Daley gives Martin the agree-to-pay documents to sign. Business completed, Martin will now be able to borrow the money he needs just by making a phone call.

The following Saturday, Martin finds another good deal on a house. He needs to borrow $6,000 to buy it. He calls his bank and requests the $6,000.

"Fine," says Mr. Daley. "We'll take $6,000, deduct it from your $14,000 operating line of credit, and deposit it in your checking account."

Now Martin is able to write out a check for $6,000 from his checking account and be sure the money will be there.

On the operating line of credit that is approved, you do not have to pay interest on a dime of that money until you give the bank a call on the phone or have them deposit that money in your checking account. If you have an operating line of credit of $14,000 and you borrow $6,000, you are paying interest on only the $6,000, not on the entire $14,000 of your operating line of credit.

A bank will charge you a service fee in the beginning to set up the operating line of credit, but it will cost you less than 1% of that total amount you are approved for. In this case, an operating line of credit valued at $14,000 would cost you less than $140 to set up in the beginning.

This gives you great confidence knowing that whenever you need to draw money in your real estate investing, you can tap into that money supply quickly.

Commercial Loan: Short-Term Note

40

Ted Wilson has found a good deal on a fixer-upper. He has bought the house at $37,000, and knows he can sell it for at least $46,000 if he paints the outside and performs minor renovations inside. He calls in a contractor who can do the whole job for $2,700.

Ted has spent what ready cash he had in buying this property and has no money left to spend in repairs.

He goes to his bank and talks with the loan officer, explaining the situation.

"Fine," says Mr. Dalton. "What you're asking for is a commercial short-term loan. We'll make the life of the loan for 90 days. At the end of 90 days you simply come in and pay us off, and that's it. It's that simple."

Of course, they check out his credit rating and the evaluation of the property he has bought. Everything checks out okay, and they approve the loan.

Ted Wilson calls in his contractor, who goes to work renovating the house, inside and out. The work takes a little over a month. The property looks great and Ted offers it for resale. He puts up a FOR SALE sign on the front lawn, which he has carefully mowed, and puts an ad in the local newspaper. He puts other ads on local bulletin boards in supermarkets.

Within two weeks, he has a buyer. The young man and his wife love the new paint on the house. The wife is particularly happy with the way he has renovated the kitchen. The man says to Ted, "Mr. Wilson, we like your place very much. We can't quite pay you the $46,000 you're asking, but we can pay you $44,000."

Ted thinks it over. "Okay, I'll settle for $44,000. But I'll need $4,000 down in cash."

"All right, we can pay you that much down."

Ted completes the sale of the house, and receives the $4,000 down in cash. He goes back to his bank and talks with the loan officer. He is repaying his loan of $2,700.

Mr. Dalton is impressed. "Well, Mr. Wilson, I see you are paying off the note a little more than a month early. You made good time on this one. Be sure to come in and see us again whenever you need cash on another one of your real estate investments."

The commercial short-term note is a work-horse in the real estate investment field. It's great for getting money quickly to fix a house up and resell it. It is all very simple. You borrow a certain amount from the bank, up to what your credit rating and the value of your property will allow, and sign a note to repay the entire amount, plus all interest due, at the end of 90 days.

Letter Of Credit 41

Tim Ryan is a young real estate investor who is just starting out. He has a steady job, but has no real working capital. He knows that his only chance at getting started in real estate investing is to buy with little or no money down, especially no money down.

Every evening after work, he checks in the newspaper ads for good deals. He has called many of them, and has gone out to see several houses for sale. He has made his no money down offer a few times, but no seller has ever accepted one of his offers. He is beginning to get a little discouraged. But, one Saturday morning, he gathers himself together, and goes out to see a house he found advertised in the paper the night before. He finds the house in a section of town near the university. He knows it would make a good rental property.

A middle-aged man opens the door. "Good morning," says Tim. "Are you Mr. Magnum?"

"Yes. And you must be Tim Ryan. Come on in, I'll show you the place."

The house is not new, but it is large. It has three bedrooms upstairs and two bedrooms down. "I've been renting the place to students from the university," Mr. Magnum explains. "The university has okayed it for two students in each bedroom. I rent it out to ten students at one time. I charge $100 a month, per student, so the place is bringing in $1,000 a month in rental income. It's a good deal, but you do have to manage the place closely. If you're interested, I'll sell you the property for $80,000."

"That's a fair enough price," Jim replies. "Will you take monthly payments on your equity?"

The seller smiles. "I have a lot of equity in this place, Tim. I own it free and clear. We're talking about $80,000 worth of equity."

"Oh."

"But I'll tell you what I'll do. I would consider monthly payments, if the monthly payments were high enough. How much would you be willing to pay per month?"

"I could handle $800 a month," says Tim. "That would be 1% per month of the total."

Mr. Magnum looks at him thoughtfully. "$800 a month would be fine. Come to my lawyer's office Monday morning at 10:00AM and we'll draw up the papers."

Tim Ryan walks out of the house floating on cloud nine! He has just succeeded in making his first real estate investment.

On Monday morning he walks into the office of Mr. Shields, Mr. Magnum's attorney.

The lawyer says, "Mr. Magnum tells me that you have made him an offer on his rental property, and he has accepted it. That is, he is willing to accept it as far as the monetary arrangements are concerned. However, there is just one thing I am concerned about. As Mr. Magnum's attorney, it is my duty to protect his security in any business arrangement. You are offering him no money down on the purchase of his rental house. You could walk away from the sale two or three months down the road, possibly in the middle of next winter, after Mr. Magnum has moved to California. We would then have to foreclose on the house and take it back. We would have the house to sell all over again. My duty is to protect Mr. Magnum from having something like this happening to him. You do see my position, don't you?"

"Yes," admits Tim. "But I wouldn't do that. I want to keep the house for a rental. I won't walk out on you."

"I'm afraid we need legal certainty of that," Mr. Shields says gently. "If you are paying something like $6,000 down in cash, we would have real assurance of your intentions. Then if you walked out of the deal, Mr. Magnum would at least have $6,000 to show for it. I would, of course, be very sure that you would do everything in your power to keep from losing your $6,000."

"I see what you mean," says Tim. "Give me two more days. Let me see what I can do."

"Agreed," says Mr. Shields. "We'll give you two more days." Tim walked out of the lawyer's office shaking his head. He's got to do something, and quick. But what? There is no way in the world he can come up with $6,000 in cash.

Tim starts talking with all the real estate investors he knows. He comes across one that says, "Tim, I think what you need is a Letter of Credit."

"Letter of Credit? What's that?"

"Go talk to your banker about that. He can explain the details of it better than I can."

Tim goes to his banker, "Mr. Dougle, I am a real estate investor. I'm just starting out and a friend of mine just told me I should find out how a Letter of Credit works."

Mr. Dougle nods. "The Letter of Credit got started in the shipping industry. Supposed a buyer in London, England wanted to buy some silks from a seller in Hong Kong. The seller in Hong Kong says 'You send me a check first, then I'll send you the silks.' The buyer in London says, 'You want me to send you a check first? You must have been drinking too much tea! You send me the silks first, and then I'll send you the check!'"

So, the banks stepped into the picture with their Letter of Credit. A bank in London checks out the buyer's credit and issues a Letter of Credit to the seller in Hong Kong, promising the seller that if the buyer in London does not come up with the money when the silks arrive in London then the bank itself will pay the seller in full for the silk.

"I'm beginning to get the idea," says Tim.

Mr. Dougle continues, "It works the same way in the real estate field. If you have a decent credit rating, this bank will issue you a Letter of Credit that you can give to a seller of real estate. If you should ever default in your mortgage payments, the bank will promise to pay the seller of the property a certain amount, whatever is written in the Letter of Credit. If you buy property and we issue the seller a Letter of Credit for $10,000, and you miss a payment on the mortgage, all that seller has to do is come in here, tell us you have missed your loan payment, and he can collect the full $10,000 by showing us the Letter of Credit."

Suddenly, Tim is not certain this is such a good idea. "Now just a minute! It looks like this Letter of Credit protects the seller against me. I am more interested in what is going to protect me from the seller! What's to prevent him from coming into the bank, showing you my Letter of Credit, and collecting $10,000?"

Mr. Dougle laughs. "Don't worry about that. Our bank will protect you. The seller has to sign an affidavit that you are behind on your mortgage payments before we pay out any money on the Letter of Credit. If he signs that affidavit falsely, he's in big legal trouble." Tim is reassured.

The following morning, he meets with Mr. Magnum in his attorney's office. He tells them both, "I have something new to add to my offer: a Letter of Credit. You said you would feel secure with a $6,000 down payment. Well, I'm getting a $6,000 Letter of Credit from the First Security Bank. If I ever try to walk out on this deal, or if I ever miss one mortgage payment, all you have to do is to take this Letter of Credit down to the bank and they'll give you the $6,000."

Mr. Shields exchanges a glance with Mr. Magnum. "If you make that Letter of Credit good for two years from the closing date of the sale, that will make us feel secure."

That does the trick! Tim Ryan has just joined the ranks of successful real estate investors.

A Letter of Credit is not hard to get, and the amount of money you can write into that letter of credit is dependent upon your personal credit standing. The bank will charge you about 1% a year on the face value of the Letter of Credit. Tim's Letter of Credit is for $6,000 for two years. It will cost him $120 in interest. The bank also charges a small service fee for the Letter of Credit.

The letter of credit works wonders in building instant trust in both the seller and the seller's attorney. When you are out making offers to buy real estate with no money down, you need to have that seller trust you, and the Letter of Credit will usually do the trick.

Second
Mortgage Crank   **42**

Randy Newell is a young man who is very interested in real estate investment. He has a steady job and looks for real estate in his spare time. He is driving through a neighborhood looking for a house that was advertised in the newspaper for sale, when he happens to see a sign which reads FOR SALE BY OWNER on a well-kept front lawn.

A short time later, he finds himself inside where Bill Jackson and his wife are showing him the interior of their home. This one is no fixer-upper. This house is in very good condition. The owners have taken good care of it in every way.

"You do have a nice home here. How much are you asking for it?"

"We had it appraised at $73,000."

"It's well worth it," says Randy. "The only trouble is, that would be a little too steep for me. Would you consider selling it for $69,000?"

Mr. and Mrs. Jackson look at each other, and Mr. Jackson says, "Yes, but there's one thing for sure. We've got to have $10,000 cash when we sell the house."

"Do you have a mortgage on the house?"

"Yes. The mortgage is $42,000, at 8% interest. The payments are $375 a month."

This is a great first mortgage! Randy knows that if he buys this house, he is going to want to retain this first mortgage. He says, "Then, can I just assume your first mortgage and make you monthly payments on your equity?"

"Yes, if you'll give us the $10,000 cash down at closing."

Randy calculates this whole deal in his mind. He does not have $10,000 cash. He will have to borrow it. If he gets a new first mortgage on the house and pays off the old first mortgage, he's going to be losing that great interest rate of 8% and those low monthly payments of $350 per month. There is no way he will give up this first mortgage.

He says to the sellers, "All right, I'll give you your $10,000 cash down for the house. But you'll have to give me a little time to raise the money. What I'm going to do is buy your home from you and then get a second mortgage on the house. A second mortgage for $10,000. Then, I'll give you that $10,000 cash as your down payment."

Molly Jackson looks a little worried. "Are you sure nothing could go wrong? We really have to have our $10,000 cash."

"Molly's right," says Mr. Jackson. "We've got to be doubly sure that we get that $10,000. If we sell you the house first, what guarantee do we have that you'll give us the $10,000 later? I hate to sound suspicious, but we've got to have some guarantee."

Randy smiles. "You'll get your guarantee, in writing! We'll write it into the purchase contract that I will have no more than 90 days to pay you that $10,000 cash. Otherwise, you'll get the house back."

The sellers exchange glances again. "Fair enough. That sounds like a good enough guarantee."

Whenever you want to buy a house which has a large first mortgage with a low interest rate, plus low monthly payments, you will want to keep this first mortgage intact. When you need to raise money for the seller, instead of taking out a new first mortgage, which is called the first mortgage crank, you will want to use this second mortgage crank: Take out this new second mortgage for only the money that you really need at the time, as in this case, the money needed to give the seller the cash down payment. Then, you give the seller back a third mortgage on the rest of his equity, getting as low an interest rate as possible on that third mortgage.

43 Created Paper

George and Gloria Malone are a middle-income couple with three children, one in high school, and the other two in elementary school. He is a landscaper and she works in the university library.

They have a fairly comfortable income, but do not have much left after they have covered all their living expenses each month. They are looking forward to the day when their children will enter college. They know they are going to need more money to help pay for their children's higher education. They are looking for a way to supplement their regular monthly income.

They are invited to attend a seminar on real estate investing. They attend the seminar. At its close, they are convinced this is the way they can acquire that needed extra income.

George and Gloria go out together and start looking for good buys in real estate investment. Every evening, they divide up the real estate section of the newspaper. He circles ads in his part and she circles ads in her part. They take turns phoning numbers listed in the ads. Whenever a house seems interesting to both of them, they go out together and look at the house.

One day, they find a house that seems ideal for their investment purposes. It is located within easy walking distance of the university.

A short time later, the Malone's complete their tour of the property. There are three bedrooms on the main floor, and a large basement with three additional rooms. Gloria thinks they too could be used as bedrooms. She mentions this to George, "We could rent this place out to the university students and put two of them in each bedroom. That would give us twelve students altogether, six upstairs and six down.

George says to the owners, "You said on the phone that you're asking $60,000 for the house. Do you have a mortgage on it?"

"Yes," says Ralph. "We have a mortgage of $40,000. It's at 9% interest and the payments are $400 a month. And it is assumable."

"Would you take monthly payments on your equity?" asks Gloria.

"Well, I don't know," says Hazel Stevens. "We hadn't thought about that."

"There's something we might do to make it better for you," says Gloria. She reaches into her purse and pulls out her pocket calculator. She makes a few calculations and says, "Yes, it would work."

"What would work?" asks George Malone, looking a little puzzled. Then, he says, "Oh! Are you thinking what I'm thinking? The equity in our own home?"

The next day George and Gloria call in a contractor to give them a bid on putting in a bathroom and a kitchen. The contractor looks the basement over and says, "The bathroom alone will cost about $2,500. The kitchen will cost you another $3,000. You'll need a stove and a refrigerator. The stove will cost you about $330, the refrigerator about $440. I would say you're looking at something like $4,500 total."

George and Gloria Malone have a real problem. They do not have $4,500 to spare.

The next morning, George says, "That does it. I'm going to look through that book we got at the real estate seminar."

He searches through the book, looking for a way of raising money for real estate deals. There are many, but he does not see one which applies to their case. Then, "Gloria, this one may be it! It's called the FHA Fix-Up Loan."

"Let's give it a try." They go to the bank together late that afternoon, and talk with the loan officer. "Mr. Donahue, we have a problem here. We've just bought a house and we want to rent it out to students. We are required to put a bathroom and a kitchen in our basement. It's going to cost about $4,000. I've been reading about this FHA fix-up loan. Would that apply in a case like this?"

Mr. Donahue nods. "Yes, the FHA fix-up loan would apply in this case. But first, we have to make sure that both you and the house qualify for the loan, that the rental income from the house is greater than your monthly loan payments. In other words, the house must be able to support itself with a full rental income. Your monthly payments should not be more than 80% of the monthly rental income from the property."

Gloria says, "The inspectors from the university thought we could reasonably charge $120 for each student on the main floor and $100 for each student in the basement. That would be $600 for the basement students and $720 for the main floor students. That would be a total of $1,320 a month."

Mr. Donahue punches the figures into his calculator. "Okay, 80% of $1,320 is $1,056. What are your mortgage payments on the house now?"

"Well," answers George, "We have $400 a month to pay on our first mortgage and on our second mortgage we're paying . . . " He looks at Gloria suddenly. "And we don't have any second mortgage on the place! We have $20,000 worth of equity in it right now."

Mr. Donahue shrugs. "You're in great shape for this FHA fix-up loan. No problem at all, as far as the house is concerned. Now what about your financial status?"

They give him their information concerning the jobs both of them have, and then they fill out a financial statement.

The bank approves the loan with no trouble. Afterward, George says, "I didn't realize what a powerful position that put us in, giving the Stevens a mortgage loan on our house, trading it for the $20,000 equity in their house. We just ended up with $20,000 equity in the Stevens' house. That really puts us in great shape.

"We'll have to remember that for future use," comments Gloria.

So, George and Gloria Malone have the bathroom and kitchen put into their basement, fill it full of students, and start collecting $1,320 a month in rent. This gives them great confidence that when the time comes for their children to go to the university, they will have enough money set aside for that purpose.

When The Seller Demands All Cash

44

Bill and Sally Langford have been married for nine years. They have two children, both in elementary school.

Sally was seriously studying the violin when she first met Bill. She always intended to take up the violin again, but had always been sidetracked, mostly because of family finances. For the last two years she has been working full time in a department store to supplement Bill's income as a high school mathematics teacher. She does not complain, but when she takes out the violin to play on it a little, Bill can see that she has deep regrets.

Bill can stand it no longer. "Sally," he says, "how about if you worked half a day at the department store? Could you get the lessons that you need for the violin at the university?"

Sally looks at him. "Oh, I'm sure that I could. But how would we manage on the finances?"

"I'm going to do something," says Bill. "I'm not sure just what, but I am going to do something!"

He goes out of the house and takes a long walk. When he comes back, he says, "I've been thinking it over, Sally. Our friends George and Gloria are really making it in real estate. Let's go talk to them and see if they can give us some ideas we can use."

They go visit the Malones and have a long talk with them.

The next day, Bill and Sally go house hunting. They don't find what they are looking for in a day, or even a week. But less than a month later, after much searching, they find a medium-sized house close to campus. They call and make an appointment to meet the owner the following afternoon. As they walk up the sidewalk to the front door, Sally whispers, "I'm nervous, Bill. I've never done anything like this before in my life."

"I know just how you feel," replies Bill. "I haven't either. We've got to start somewhere."

He adds, "Remember, this is for your career as a violinist."

At this, Sally raises her chin slightly and punches the doorbell with her finger. The door opens, "Hello, I'm Sally Langford, and this is my husband, Bill. Are you Mr. Wilson?"

The elderly man replies, "Yes, I've been expecting you." He gestures for them to come inside. "I rent the place to students," Mr. Wilson explains.

"Oh, really?" asks Sally. "This is what we would like to do with it. How many students does the university allow you to have here?"

"Ten. There are three bedrooms upstairs and two bedrooms in the basement. You can have two students in each bedroom."

He takes them down into the basement, and they see that it is fully finished, with two bedrooms, a bathroom, and a kitchen.

"This is just what we've been looking for," Sally says.

"I'm asking $60,000 for the house. I have an assumable mortgage of $24,000. My equity is $34,000. One thing I should tell you is that I have already had several offers to pay monthly payments on the equity, but I turned them down. I need all cash for my equity."

One look at the seller's set face is enough to convince Bill and Sally that he's not kidding. "Okay, Mr. Wilson," says Bill. "We'll get you your full equity of $36,000."

Sally looks at him as though she thinks he has just lost his mind. "How?" she whispers to him urgently.

"I'm not just sure yet," he admits. "But I know I'm going to do it." He sits down at one of the desks provided in the basement apartment for the students. He pulls out his calculator and goes to work. He talks to Sally and Mr. Wilson as he makes his calculations. "This house is worth $60,000. You can finance up to 80% of that, which is $48,000. It already has a $24,000 mortgage on it, so subtract that out, and that leaves $24,000 of equity that we could give in cash if we put a second mortgage on it." He looks up a Mr. Wilson. "We would give you that $24,000 on your equity."

"All right so far," says Mr. Wilson. "You've paid me $24,000 of my $36,000 equity. That leaves $12,000. Can you come up with that other $12,000?"

"Yes, we can," says Bill. "We own our own home, and it is worth $50,000. We have a mortgage of $26,000 on it. That gives us an equity of $24,000. We can borrow up to 80% of its $50,000 value, which is $40,000. Subtract the $26,000 first mortgage we have on our house now, and that gives us $16,000 that we can borrow on a second mortgage. We'll borrow $12,000 on that second mortgage, and give it to you for the rest of your equity.

We'll be giving you the $24,000 from the second mortgage on your own house here, and the other $12,000 from the second mortgage on our home. That adds up to your $36,000 equity. There may be two or three thousand dollars closing costs; I'm not sure. But we have $4,000 more we can borrow on the second mortgage on our home. It looks like we can buy your house, Mr. Wilson, and pay you your $36,000 cash."

"Indeed," agrees Mr. Wilson. "You're a very resourceful young man."

The following day, Sally quits her job at the department store and enrolls in a private violin class at the university. The rental income from the house they have just bought will help to make her dreams come true.

45   Created Paper Two

Ted and Sarah Corey have been married for 14 years. They have three children, one in junior high school, and the other two in elementary school. He is a computer repairman and she works part time in a clothing store. They have decided that they have to build for their own future, and for the future of their children.

One day, Ted repairs a computer in the office of a real estate investor, who uses his computer for his investment business. Ted programs computers to some degree, and becomes interested in the computer programs used by this individual. In going over these programs with the investor, he becomes convinced that real estate is the way to build for his future, and for the future of his family.

He goes home and talks with Sarah and she agrees that real estate might very well be the foundation of their future.

Ted has learned some things from this real estate investor, and he sets forth to try some of them out. He reads the newspaper ads diligently, checking out the few that look good to him. He finds one that really interests him. It is a respectable, single-family dwelling in a quiet neighborhood. He talks to the owner. "How much do you want for your home, Mr. Bradshaw?"

"It was appraised at $62,500."

"Does it have an assumable mortgage?"

"Yes," replies Mr. Bradshaw, "It has a mortgage of $28,000."

"Will you take monthly payments on your equity? I'll pay 1% per month on your total equity, and give you 12% interest on it."

Mr. Bradshaw hesitates. "I'd be willing to take some of my equity in monthly payments, but not all of it. I would feel better if you put some money down, so I will know you have actually bought some interest in it."

"Would you be willing to lower the price to $60,000 if I did that?"

"Maybe."

"This is what I would like to do, Mr. Bradshaw. I have a house that's worth $65,000, and it has a mortgage on it of $34,000. This gives me an equity of $31,000. I can borrow up to 80% of the value of the house, and 80% of $65,000 is $52,000. I already have a mortgage on it of $34,000, so with a second mortgage on my house, in the form of an $18,000 mortgage note, I will be buying $18,000 into your house. Would that make you feel secure?"

The seller laughs, "Yes, I guess it would at that."

"And, if you sell me your house at $60,000, and it has a $28,000 assumable mortgage, that gives you an equity of $32,000. I'm buying into your $32,000 equity with my $18,000 mortgage note. That leaves $14,000 of your equity that I still owe you. I'll give you a second mortgage note on your house in the amount of $14,000 to cover your last $14,000 worth of equity. I'll pay you 1% per month on each mortgage note, or 12% interest."

Mr. Bradshaw nods, "I see what you're talking about. I'll go along with your offer. It's a deal." There is only one thing left for Ted to do. He has to go home and tell Sarah that he's going to put a second mortgage on their home.

"No!" exclaims Sarah. "We're not going to put a second mortgage on our home! I'm not going to jeopardize our future and the future of the children."

"Let's talk about the future, Sarah. We agreed this real estate investment business looked like the best thing we could possibly do to build a long-term financial future, didn't we?"

"But isn't there some safer way of doing it than mortgaging our home? We don't want to lose everything we've got in some wild real estate gamble."

"No, we don't." Ted agrees. "But this isn't really a gamble. We'll be paying 1% per month on a total of $32,000, and that's $320 a month. His first mortgage is at $260 a month, that adds up to $580 a month on the house we're buying right now. The rents keep going up about 5% each year, but our monthly payments on the house will never change."

"Another thing, if things got tight, we could always put the house up for resale, and make a quick profit on it. As far as losing our home is concerned, the second mortgage we'll be giving him is only $18,000. The payments on that are $180 per month. If everything about the other house fell through and we lost everything on that property, we would still be obligated to pay only $180 a month on that second mortgage. No one could ever take our home away from us."

Sarah brightens considerably. "Yes, I see what you mean now. I think real estate is going to make it possible for us to live that future we've always talked about."

Created Paper Three   **46**

Paul and Alice Jordan have two children in elementary school and a nice home near the university community. Alice is president of the Literary Society which meets at the university every month. They are happy in their lives, but desire to build a solid financial foundation for the future. Not only do they want to provide a higher education for their children, but would like to publish their own volumes of Private Edition Literature books.

They decide that before they would be able to enter into any publishing venture, they would first have to establish some sort of supplemental income. However, they are not yet sure what that source of income might be. One day, a student in one of Paul's American Literature classes is telling him his troubles. "I just found out that my roommates and I may be evicted at any time! If he sells the house now, we might all have to move out in the middle of the semester."

"I can understand how you must feel," says Paul. He paces back and forth across his office, thinking. "Why don't you give me the name, address and phone number of your landlord. I think I'll go and have a chat with him."

Andy looks somewhat relieved. "Thank you, Dr. Jordan. We would all appreciate anything you can do." Paul calls the landlord and arranges to meet him at the house where the students are living. Mr. Jamieson, the owner, is cordial to him.

"I appreciate your concern for the students, Dr. Jordan, but there's no real problem, at least not until the end of the semester. The university standard rental agreement states that both the student and the landlord are bound to a lease which can only be terminated at the conclusion of a semester. No matter who buys this place, all the students living in the house have the right to remain here until the end of the semester. I didn't know any of them were worried, or I would have mentioned it to them sooner."

Paul smiles a little. "Apparently, they didn't read the contract they signed at the beginning of the school year."

Mr. Jamieson laughs, "Yes, the students won't have any problem, at least until the end of the semester. Of course, the new owner might ask them to leave at the end of that time." Then he sobers. "I'm the one with the real problem. I'm in a bind financially and have to sell this place and get some ready cash quickly."

"How much cash do you need right now?" asks Paul.

"I need $12,000 cash as quickly as I can get it."

Paul looks thoughtfully around the house. "How much are you asking for you place, Mr. Jamieson?"

"$72,000. It has an assumable mortgage of $32,000. That gives me an equity of $40,000."

"And what is your total rental income each month from the house?"

"$1,400 when it is filled. We haven't had any trouble filling it because it's so close to the university."

"I just might buy your house, Mr. Jamieson. Give me a couple of days to study this thing out. I'll get back to you." Mr. Jamieson nods.

Paul goes home and talks with Alice. They agree to go into real estate investment. They both spend the next two days researching the field of real estate investment, checking out every book in the university library on the subject, and talking with bankers, realtors, and real estate investors.

At the end of two days, Paul and Alice meet with the seller. "We found a way to get you your $12,000 in cash," says Paul. "We don't have that much cash available ourselves, but we can get it for you. What we plan to do is this. We'll buy your house, assume the $32,000 mortgage, and put a new mortgage on it, a second mortgage, for $15,000. We can do that because we can borrow up to 80% of the $72,000 value of the house and 80% of that is $57,600. Since it already has a $32,000 mortgage, we don't want to borrow any more on that second mortgage than we have to. We'll write into the purchase contract that we'll give you your $12,000 cash within 90 days of the closing date. Is that agreeable with you?"

"Yes, it is, as long as I know I'm going to get the $12,000, 90 days is fine."

Paul continues, "We're borrowing $15,000, so we'll have $3,000 left over for the closing costs. You have $40,000 equity in your house. After we pay you the $12,000 cash, you'll have $28,000 left in your equity. We could give you a $28,000 third mortgage note for the rest of your equity."

The seller looks uneasy. "I'm not sure about that. That would make this house 100% financed. You'd be assuming the first mortgage, taking out a second mortgage to give me the $12,000, and giving me a third mortgage note for the rest of my equity. You wouldn't really be putting any of your own money into it."

Paul is prepared for this. He started out by making the offer he would like to have accepted. Now that his most desired offer has been rejected, he is ready with his second offer. "All right, then, Mr. Jamieson. I can see how you feel about that situation. Let's do it this way. We own our own home, and it's worth $67,000. We have a $47,000 mortgage on it. This gives us an equity of $20,000. We'll give you a second mortgage note for $15,000 secured by the equity in our own home. Your $28,000 equity minus our second mortgage note for $15,000 will leave you $13,000 equity. Then we can give you a $13,000 mortgage note on the equity in this property. We'll actually be buying $15,000 worth of equity in your house when we buy it."

Mr. Jamieson brightens considerably. "I like this idea much better."

They make the transaction successfully. Paul and Alice Jordan decide that real estate really is going to be their means for assuring their children's future education and for publishing their own works of literature.

47   VA And FHA Loans Two

Terry Fielding is a combat veteran. He has served his country by sleeping in muddy fox holes and crawling through machine gunfire. He was wounded twice.

Now, all of that is behind him. He wants to settle down and live a peaceful, normal life as a civilian in a free country. His life has changed dramatically for the better since he met Cindy.

They married four months ago, and they are living in a small rented apartment near the university. He is working full time assembling computers, and taking a few classes at night in computer design. His professional ambition is to become a computer designer, and have his own computer company some day.

That's all in the future. Right now, he has to settle down to earning a living to provide for himself and his young wife.

One evening, Cindy says, "Terry, have you thought about owning our own home someday?"

"Yes, I've thought about it. It seems like a pretty good idea, someday."

Cindy speaks with more urgency, "This apartment is nice, but I'd really like to be in our own home *now*."

They start looking in the newspaper ads under HOUSES FOR SALE. They look at several over a period of three months until they find what they have been looking for. It's a modest little "starter home" not far from the university or from Terry's place of work.

"This is it," says Cindy. "This is where I'd like to live."

They go inside the house and talk with the owner. "How much would you like for your house, Mr. Johnson?" asks Cindy.

"$45,000," says Mr. Johnson. "It has an assumable mortgage of $23,000, at 13% interest. The monthly payments are $320 a month. I have $22,000 equity in the place and I would like that in cash at closing."

Terry looks into Cindy's face and sees her look of hopelessness. He says to the seller, "We can't afford that much right now. Could you possibly come down to the area of $41,000?"

"I would settle for $42,000, but, as I said, I do have to have my equity in cash."

The house is not large, but it does have three bedrooms and a partial basement. It seems like a comfortable place to live and start a family. Terry and Cindy like the home very much, and don't want to give up on it.

"Mr. Johnson, we'd like to buy your place, if we can afford it. Will you hold it for a week while we try to raise the money?"

"Okay, I'll give you a week, but I'll require $100 in earnest money."

Terry and Cindy go to the bank the following afternoon and talk with the loan officer, Mr. Briggs. They explain the situation to him in detail. Terry ends by asking, "Is there any way you can help us buy the house?"

"I'll do my best. First we'll have to have a full financial statement, including your regular income. We have to qualify you as buyers. If you qualify, the bank will probably lend you up to 80% on the house you want to buy."

Cindy looks dismayed. "Eighty percent won't be enough! We don't have 20% of $42,000 in cash. That would be $8,400. Isn't there any way the bank could lend us more on the house?"

"Well," says Mr. Briggs, "There is one kind of loan that will let you borrow 100% of the value of the house you're buying. That's the VA loan." He looks at Terry.

"Would you qualify as a veteran?"

Terry nods. "He was wounded twice in combat," says Cindy.

"Then that's good enough for me," says Mr. Briggs. "Bring in your Separation Papers and we'll put through a VA loan for 100% financing."

This gives Terry and Cindy Fielding a loan for $42,000 to purchase the house. They use the $42,000 cash to pay off the existing mortgage of $23,000 and give $22,000 in cash to Mr. Johnson for his equity.

Terry and Cindy are getting a real bargain on this VA loan, and they know it. The old first mortgage on this house was at 13% interest. The new VA loan has an interest rate of only $11\frac{1}{2}\%$.

The VA is simply the king of all loans! If you are a veteran, and if you are going to live in the house yourself, you are eligible for one of these VA loans to buy your own home. The VA loan is definitely the best way to go.

Section 6

Partnerships

Partnerships

You can get into some great deals if you go into property ownership with one or more people. One partner may have the knowledge of buying and selling property while the other partner may have the finances, or there may be a combination of these in all partners. Either way, if you partner up with the right people, you could get in on some great deals.

In some cases, one partner has all the knowledge and the other partner has all the cash.

What if you know someone who has the cash and the desire, but has been burned by being hooked up with partners in the past? That's when you can set up a deal where your "partner" has only her name on the title, but you set up an agreement with her to secure a one-half interest on an option to buy. It gives you the option to buy one-half of the interest in the property within a given number of years at its present value. It gives you the opportunity to have a vested interest in the house, keep your co-buyer happy and interested, and you will see a profit on the appreciation of the house when it comes time to sell the house to a new buyer.

Consider your spouse as your partner too if you both work well together on big purchases like real estate properties. One spouse could be available to ask the seller all the necessary questions. This could very well help the seller to be more relaxed and confident about the negotiating process.

Does your potential partner have a high cash income and high credit rating? Does she have any cash left over at the end of the month? It's possible that her high credit rating could be used instead of cash when you're negotiating with a seller. Be sure to make it well worth her benefit though. I suggest giving her 100% of all the depreciation on the properties and 50% of the appreciation. Later in this section, one of the scenarios will show you what our eager friend Randy does on such a setup with a wealthy doctor in his town.

Their Money, But Your Time And Talent

48

Randy Jones is a discouraged man. He has no money, no friends, and no influence. At least this is the way he feels sometimes. He has no equity in any property, and he owns no car. He owns nothing of any real value that he can think of. He has a part-time job that does not pay him too well. His credit rating is absolutely zilch.

He is trudging along in the rain late one dismal afternoon, feeling very down in the mouth about the world.

His stroll has taken him down a residential street where he sees a FOR SALE sign on the front lawn of a house. He peers at the house through the rain, wondering idly how much money the house would cost, if he had the money to buy it.

He doesn't.

He walks on, getting wetter by the minute. He has no coat or hat, and wishes he could find shelter somewhere.

Suddenly, he turns back and walks up the sidewalk to the house for sale. He knocks on the door, wanting to get out of the rain more than anything else. He has no hope of buying anything at this point in his life. The door opens and a tall, slender man is standing there. "Yes?"

Randy hesitates. "Uh . . . well, may I just take a look at your house? Your sign out in the yard says it's for sale."

"Sure, come on in."

Mr. Thompson, the owner, shows him through the house. At first, Randy's only real interest in the house is a temporary shelter from the rain, but as he becomes warmer and dryer, he begins to see the possibilities of owning a house like this. If he owned this house, maybe he could rent it out and bring in a profit every month. "How much do you want for your house, Mr. Thompson?"

"$60,000. $32,000 of that is my mortgage to the bank, which is assumable, and the other $28,000 is equity."

Randy feels dismayed at this. "Well, I sure don't have $28,000 in cash lying around. Thanks for showing me your house anyway, Mr. Thompson. It was nice of you."

On the walk home, something inside Randy starts to click. He drops into a bank and inquires about getting a loan to buy the house. The loan officer is polite, but Randy soon gets the message. He doesn't have enough credit to buy a bicycle!

Randy leaves the bank thinking, "There must be a better way."

After supper, he goes to the public library and finds a number of books on real estate investment. He finds things in these books which surprise and encourage him. The next day, he goes to the office of Mr. Van Fleet, the owner of the big department store where he works part-time. The secretary says to him, "What do you want to talk to Mr. Van Fleet about?"

Randy feels embarrassed. "Oh, just a little business I want to discuss with him."

"Because, if it's about a raise," the secretary eyes him significantly, "forget it. He's in no mood to give raises to anyone lately."

Randy sweats it out in the outer office until Mr. Van Fleet is ready for him. "What can I do for you today, Randy?"

Randy gathers up his courage and begins. "Mr. Van Fleet, would you be interested in a deal that would save you money on your income tax?"

Mr. Van Fleet's face does strange things at the mention of the word "taxes."

"Sit down, Randy, and tell me what you have in mind."

"Sir, did you know whenever you invest in a piece of property you can declare the whole value of the building on that property over a period of 15 years? In other words, if you bought a piece of land that had a building on it valued at $150,000 right now, you could declare that whole $150,000 as deductions on your income taxes over a 15 year period? That means you would be able to deduct one-fifteenth of the value of the building every year from your net taxable income."

Mr. Van Fleet nods. "Yes, Randy, I'm aware of that."

Randy continues, "The property will really be appreciating in value every year. That depreciation is just on paper. Actually, the value of the property will be going up on the average of 10% a year. You'd make $15,000 just on appreciation in the first year."

Mr. Van Fleet looks impressed. "I'm aware of that too, Randy. The only reason I have not invested heavily in real estate is that I can't manage that much real estate and still manage my own department store. I tried investing in real estate some years ago, and found out it just didn't work for me. I was spending so much time and energy in managing the real estate I did not have enough time left to manage my own business. I started losing out on both my real estate investments and my department store. I decided I had to choose one or the other. I chose my department store and reluctantly sold my real estate investments."

"What if you could have both?" asks Randy. "I would be willing to go out and look for good deals in real estate for you, and then manage them after you buy them. You have the money to invest and I have the talent and the energy to manage the real estate. I'll take care of all the rentals and the maintenance. You could have all the depreciation on the buildings. At this stage of the game, I don't worry about needing big tax deductions. I would, however, like half of the appreciation on the property and whatever profit there is in the rental income after we deduct the monthly payments on the property."

"All right, I'll give you your chance. Find a property for sale, get as good a deal on it as you can, and then come back to me for my final approval on it. I'll provide the down payment that's needed. You keep the property rented so there will be cash flow coming in every month from the property. I'll let you keep whatever profit there is in the monthly rental. We'll share the appreciation 50/50 when and if we resell the property. What I'm after here is mainly the appreciation. I can use some good-sized tax deductions."

49   Using The Option To Buy To Split The Benefits

Randy Jones is making good on his real estate investments and rental managing. He is doing fine with Mr. Van Fleet, but he is becoming more ambitious now, and is on the lookout for another partner.

Another partner with money!

One afternoon he goes into a restaurant for a hamburger. The place is called "Esther and Irv's." As he eats, he notices the name "Irv" on the hat of the chef, and the name "Esther" on the hat of the waitress. "This is a delicious hamburger. Could you put another one on for me?"

"I'm glad you like it," says Irv. "Hamburgers and steaks are my specialties."

"From the names on your hats," says Randy, "you must be the owners. How's business?"

"Great!" grins Irv. "My hamburgers are very popular in this part of town."

"I can see why," says Randy.

As he eats, he sees many customers coming in ordering hamburgers. He observes a lot of money going over the counter.

He decides that even a small business can be very successful bringing in a lot of cash for the owner. He begins to think about Esther and Irv as possible new partners for his real estate ventures.

"Have you ever considered the benefits of investing in real estate?" he asks. Irv looks surprised. "Yes, sometimes. Our restaurant keeps us pretty busy, though."

Randy proceeds to explain the tax benefits and the appreciation gain in real estate investment. He ends by saying, "I'm a real estate investor, and I'm looking for partners. If you put up the cash for the down payment, we can share the appreciation 50/50. I'll handle all the management, including all the work in renting the various properties. I keep any profit that comes in on the rental income minus the operating and monthly property expenses. Does that sound fair enough?"

Irv hesitated. "He's remembering the first, last, and the only partner we ever had in business," Esther said. "He came into our restaurant as a partner, and ended up by taking it over and pretty well kicked us out of our own business. We had to start all over again. We haven't forgotten that."

Irv agrees. "You look like a nice guy, but there are just too many things that can go wrong in a partnership. Your deal looks good, I'll say that. But we don't want to go into partnership with anybody again for any reason. Sorry."

Randy has been buying and reading all the books on real estate investments he can lay his hands on. He knows just how to handle this situation. "If that's what's bothering you, I have a proposal that I think you'll really like. It's called the option to buy. This is the way it works. You put up the cash for the down payment, and you get the deed to the property all in your name. I'm not on there anywhere, so it's not a partnership at all."

Irv and Esther look puzzled at this. "But how will that do you any good?" asks Irv.

"Because when you buy that house and get it in your name, part of the deal is that you sign an agreement with me called an option to buy. It will give me the option to buy one-half interest in that property within so many years, say 10 or 20."

"I still don't see how that will do you any good," says Irv. "What good would it do you to have the right to buy the house sometime in the future?"

"Because you agree to sell me the house at one-half of its present value. This means that I will have half of the appreciation value of the house over the years. In other words, if we sell the house in five years at a selling price of $20,000 more than you paid for it now, I would see my option to buy one-half interest in the house at today's price. I would pay you one-half of your purchase price for the house, and my one-half interest in the house when we sold it would bring $10,000 profit for my one-half interest."

"Sure, I can see what you're talking about now. That way, Esther and I hold the title to the property, but you still have your half interest in it."

"Right."

"Suppose Esther and I want to sell the house some day and you don't? What happens then?"

"No problem," answered Randy. "You go ahead and sell. I would just keep my option to buy one-half interest in the house at today's price, no matter how high the value of the house had risen at the time you were selling the house. The house could be sold two or three times, and I would still have my right to sell my option to buy one-half interest at any time to someone else. You would still have the full title to the house, and could keep the house as long as you wanted, or sell it whenever you wanted, no matter who held the option to buy the one-half interest in the house."

Irv leans across the counter. "This sounds like an okay deal! Count us in."

Using Credit Instead Of Cash 50

The more successful Randy Jones becomes as a real estate investor, the more he wants to do in real estate. He is always on the lookout now for new investors, because he realizes that the more investors he has to work with, the quicker he can put a deal together when he finds a good one. He has a car now, and as he is driving across town to find the address of a house advertised in the newspaper for sale, he passes a large, impressive Doctor's building. There is a big parking lot behind it filled with cars.

Randy takes a good look and notices many of these cars look expensive. If clients like these are going to see the doctor, then maybe Randy should go see the doctor, too.

He swings his car into the parking lot and goes inside the building. He approaches the receptionist behind the front desk.

"Have you been here before?" she asks.

"No," says Randy.

"Then fill out these forms, and sit down and wait until I call your name."

"To tell you the truth, I'm not really a patient. I don't need any medical attention. I just need a few minutes to speak to Dr. Sorenson. I'll only be a few minutes."

The receptionist smiles, but shakes her head. "I'm sorry, that would be impossible. Dr. Sorenson is very busy today."

"Could you give him a note from me?"

The receptionist looks surprised.

Randy writes a note on the receptionist's pad. It says, "Dr. Sorenson, I can save you some big money on your income taxes. Please let me know if you are interested. Signed, Randy Jones."

He folds the note carefully, slips it inside an envelope at the desk, and hands it to the receptionist. She looks at him strangely, but takes the note and goes through the door at the back of the receptionist's office.

In a few minutes, she returns, looking at him even more strangely. "Dr. Sorenson will see you on his lunch break at one o'clock."

Randy said, "Tell him I'll be back to see him then."

When one o'clock comes, Dr. Sorenson welcomes Randy returning into his office. "Well, Mr. Jones, I would like to talk to you about this message you have for reducing my income taxes. If it works, I'm interested."

"It works," said Randy. "I'm a real estate investor and I can give you all the tax shelter you need. If you'll put up the cash for me to use as down payments on various real estate deals, I'll give you all the depreciation on the buildings on the properties. For this service, I get half of the appreciation, and whatever profit comes from renting the properties to tenants."

Dr. Sorenson looks interested. "I can see how that would work. But I have a problem. I don't have any cash to use in down payments on properties."

Randy stares at him in disbelief. "What? Why, all of this office . . . "

"I know, I know," agrees Dr. Sorenson. "I do have a really high income. The trouble is, I have high expenses too. I'm afraid my wife and I have some expensive tastes, and at the present time, we're spending the money as fast as it's coming in. It seems that the harder I work and the more money comes in, the more bills we have to pay. I just don't have any available cash to use for down payments on real estate. If I did, I would certainly accept your offer."

Randy is ready for this one. He has not only been reading all the books he can find on real estate, but has also recently attended a good real estate seminar, where he was able to ask questions directly and get some good answers. He has learned a very valuable technique which applies perfectly here. He says, "Don't worry about that, Dr. Sorenson. If you really want in on this deal, we can still make it work, even if you don't have any ready cash to use for down payments."

"Really? How?"

"You bring in a lot of cash every month as a doctor, don't you?"

"Yes I do. My problem is that I never have any cash left."

"That doesn't make much difference when you're filling out a financial statement, and you're putting down your average monthly income. If you have a high regular monthly income, then you have a high credit rating. And, a high credit rating can be used effectively instead of cash when you're buying property."

Dr. Sorenson leans back in his chair. "Hmmm . . . I don't have the time to go out looking for real estate, and I certainly don't have the time to manage the real estate after it's bought."

"You won't have to worry about beating the bushes, looking for property to buy. I'll take care of that. After we buy it, I'll take care of all the management, including the rentals. All I need from you is your high credit rating. For that, you'll get 100% of the depreciation on the buildings we buy, and 50% of all the appreciation as the price of the property goes up year by year."

Dr. Sorenson looks satisfied. "Yes, I'd like an arrangement like that. When can we start?"

"We can start with the property I was looking for when I found you instead."

51   Using Your Partner's Equity Instead Of Your Cash

Randy Jones continues to go out looking for good deals and buying property. One day, he checks out a house that has been advertised in the newspaper. He locates the house in a quiet suburban neighborhood. The house looks in good condition. He walks up to the door and rings the bell. A middle-aged man answers the door. Randy says, "Hi, are you Mr. Travis? I've come to see the house you have for sale."

"Of course. Come on in."

Mrs. Travis joins them in the living room. "I'm sure you'll like our home. We hate to sell it, really."

"Oh, why are you selling it?"

Mr. Travis explains, "Well, we've been seeing the values of property going up and up, and we see that our house has been making a lot of money over the past years. We'd like to get some of that money in cash instead of having it all tied up in the house. We finally decided to sell it."

"We have mixed feelings about this," adds Mr. Travis. "We'd like some extra cash, but we also like our house. It was a hard decision for us, deciding to put the house on the market."

"How much is your house worth now?" asked Randy.

"We had it appraised at $64,000," replies Mr. Travis.

"Do you have an assumable mortgage on the house?"

"Yes, a small one. It's at $18,000 right now."

"That gives you a lot of equity," comments Randy. He takes out his pocket calculator. "That gives you an equity of $46,000. That's the equity you'd like to turn into cash, right?"

"Right."

"Well," says Randy, "I can see that I can't handle a $46,000 cash deal right now. However, I've got another appointment in 45 minutes, so I've got to leave. I'll keep your house in mind, and if I can come up with something that would be suitable for both you and me, I'll get back with you."

Randy leaves and goes out to his next appointment. It is a ten-unit apartment building near the university. He talks with the owner/manager, Mr. Tippets, who takes him on a tour of the property. All the units are occupied, most of them by students. The place seems to be in good condition, and Randy can see there will be no trouble keeping the building filled with tenants.

"How much are you asking for your apartment building, Mr. Tippetts?"

"$140,000," replies Mr. Tippetts.

"Do you have an assumable mortgage?"

"Yes, for $104,000. I have an equity of $36,000."

"Will you take monthly payments on your equity?" asks Randy.

"Well, I would, if I could get a big enough down payment. I'd like at least $15,000 in cash."

Randy runs through a checklist in his mind of how he could come up with $15,000 cash to buy this apartment building. He recalls something one of the speakers said in a real estate investment seminar he attended. "Mr. Tippetts, there might be another way to do this. Instead of giving you $15,000 in cash on your $36,000 equity, how would you like to have a $40,000 second mortgage note on a very fine home, which the owners are living in. This husband and wife really love their home, and if you hold this second mortgage on it, I can guarantee you that the monthly payments will be made to you on time."

Mr. Tippetts comments, "That's probably true. But if they did start missing payments, through some unforeseen reason, then I would be able to foreclose on their home, but not on my apartment building. I would be out if I let you buy my equity that way."

"Yes," says Randy. "I hadn't thought of that. Let's do it this way. We'll leave you $1,000 equity in your apartment building here. We'll give you one blanket mortgage covering both the second mortgage on the Travis home and the $1,000 equity you would still have in your apartment building. If something happens and we can't make payments to you any more, you can foreclose not only on the Travis home, but on your apartment building."

Mr. Tippetts nods. "That sounds like a very secure deal. I'll go along with that."

Randy goes back to talk to Mr. and Mrs. Travis. He tells them, "I have a way that can bring you in a regular monthly income without your having to sell your home to get it. Are you interested?"

Mr. and Mrs. Travis look at each other. "Indeed we are."

Randy explains the whole program to them. "I've worked out all the mathematics and the regular monthly income from the rentals will give us a good monthly profit over and above the monthly payments we'll be making to Mr. Tippetts. I'll manage the apartment building, and you and I will share the profits 50/50 on the rental income minus the monthly payments for the apartment building. I'll give you half the depreciation on the property and also half the appreciation as it increases in value. And if we ever sell the place, you'll get half the profits from that." Mr. Travis agreed, and another successful investment was made.

Using Your Partner's Personal Property Instead Of Cash

52

Randy Jones is once again driving around on the west side of town, looking for the address of a house for sale in that area. As he drives along the street, he notices a beautiful boat sitting on a trailer out on the front lawn of a house on the corner. There is a big red and white FOR SALE sign on the boat.

Randy is always looking for good deals, whether it's a house, or anything else. He pulls over to the curb and stops. He goes up to the house and knocks on the door. A lady answers.

"Hi, I'm Randy Jones. I see you have a boat for sale."

"Oh, let me call my husband." She disappears back into the house for a moment and comes back with her husband.

Her husband shakes hands with Randy. "Hello, I'm Clarence Vikers. Marsha tells me you're interested in our boat."

"Yes, I'd like to know how much you're asking for it." Mr. Vikers hesitates for a moment. "Well, four years ago I paid $20,000 for it. I haven't really used it all that much, especially in the last two or three years. The same boat would cost $26,000, brand new. I'll tell you what I'll do. I'll make you a really good deal on it. If you want it, I'll let it go at $15,000."

"All right," says Randy. "I'll keep that in mind." He turns and starts to leave. Mr. Vikers calls after him, "Actually, I haven't thought much about selling it lately. I just put the sign on it and forgot about it. If you're really interested, I'd sell it for $12,000 cash."

"All right," says Randy. "I'll write down your name and address in my notebook here."

He walks out to his car and drives off in search of the house he saw for sale somewhere in the neighborhood.

He finds it and starts talking to the owners, Mr. and Mrs. DeSpain. After seeing the property, Randy determines it will do as either a rental or a quick resale. He asks the price and Mrs. DeSpain says, "The place was appraised at $67,500. We're offering it for sale at $65,000."

"Fair enough," says Randy. "How much of that is mortgage and how much is equity."

"We have a $46,500 mortgage on it, and that's assumable. I checked. Since we are selling the house at $65,000, that gives us an equity of $18,500. We'd like as much of that in cash as possible."

"Oh, why is that?"

Mrs. DeSpain replies, "George has just received a really good job offer in California, so we're leaving this area altogether. We'll be a long way away from here, and would rather not bother with monthly payments."

"I see," said Randy. "Tell me, what part of California are you going to? Will you be near the ocean?"

Mrs. DeSpain smiles brightly. "Oh, yes, right on the ocean! We'll be living right in Santa Cruz."

Randy is getting good at the real estate game now, and he has a real inspiration. "Do you think you'll be doing some swimming and boating out there?"

"You bet your life!"

"In that case," says Randy, "I have a real deal for you. How would you like to have a 20 foot cabin cruiser valued at $20,000 for your $18,500 equity in your house?"

"Yes! I'd certainly be interested in that," says Mrs. DeSpain.

"And," says Randy, "there's even a trailer included.

"Let's take it, George! With all that ocean out there, you know we'll want to go boating. It would be a shame to live right on the ocean and not have a boat."

Mr. DeSpain has still not made up his mind. "That's true. But we could wait until we move out, and wait until we get settled in, before we think about a boat."

Randy says, "Yes, you could do that. But you will also pay a much larger price for the same boat out in California. The prices on boats will be a lot more expensive out there."

That does the trick. "All right," says Mr. DeSpain, "You just talked me into it. Of course," he adds, "I'll want to see the boat first."

"You'll like it," Randy says, "It's really a beautiful boat."

Randy hops in his car and returns to the Vikers' home—and the boat.

Mr. Vikers is surprised and happy to see Randy. "I didn't expect to see you back so soon. Have you thought some more about my boat?"

"I sure have," Randy assures him. "I have a deal I think you will really like. I'm a real estate investor. If you want to become partners with me on buying a fine house not far from here, I've arranged it so we can use your boat as a down payment on the property. You will have a half interest in the house, and I'll manage the real estate end of it. I'll take care of renting the house until it's time to resell it at a profit. Then I'll share the profits with you 50/50. You'll get half the appreciation in the house, and also have half the depreciation. You can take that depreciation off your taxes."

Mrs. Vikers whispers to him, "Take it, Clarence! You're never going to get rid of that boat otherwise."

Mr. Vikers needs no urging from his wife. He says, "It's a deal."

Less than half an hour later, Randy drives up to the DeSpain house pulling the boat behind his car. When the DeSpains come to the door, he says, "I've brought you your new boat. How do you like it?"

"What a beautiful boat!" cries Mrs. DeSpain.

Mr. DeSpain nods. "Yes. All right, Mr. Jones, you've got yourself a deal."

53 Using Your Partner's Work And Personal Property Instead Of Money

Mike Dugan has more muscles than money. He works hard enough, but never seems to get ahead. He works part-time loading and unloading trucks and freight cars. If he doesn't want to end up an old man doing this kind of work, he's got to do something now.

He sees a real estate seminar advertised in the newspaper. It says, "Real estate investment is a way to secure your financial future." He attends the seminar, buys a couple of real estate investment books, takes them home, and reads them diligently.

One day, he goes out to try his luck. First, he reads through the ads in the newspapers and circles a few that interest him. He calls and makes appointments to see the places.

Of the first three he views, the owners want cash for their equity. He comes back feeling a little discouraged.

He has one more appointment for this evening. Upon arrival for his appointment, he is pleasantly surprised by this one. He talks to the owners, Mr. and Mrs. Kempton. "You have a nice home here. How much are you asking for it?"

"$62,000," replies the seller. "It has a $41,000 mortgage, with $21,000 worth of equity."

Mike has paid careful attention at the real estate seminar, and has been reading from the books every evening. He says, "Will you take monthly payments on your equity?"

"I'm willing to take monthly payments, as long as I can get $4,000 cash down for my equity," replies Mr. Kempton.

"That sounds fair enough," says Mike. "The trouble is, I just don't have $4,000 in cash right now."

There is a deep, awkward silence. Then Mike says, "Were you going to use that $4,000 for some special purpose?"

"Yes," says Mrs. Kempton. "We need that $4,000 to get moved to Fresno, California. I've called a couple of moving agencies and that's what it's going to cost to get moved out there. The money down on the sale of the house is our only way of getting the money we need to make our move."

Now, Mike Dugan has a body packed with muscles. But that does not mean that he is all muscle and no brain. He has a brain, and he proceeds to use it.

He has not been loading and unloading trucks without learning something about it. He says, "I'll tell you what I'll do. For $4,000, I'll move you out to Fresno. I load and unload trucks all the time. I'm not asking you for $4,000 cash for this; all I'm asking is for you to give me $4,000 credit as a down payment on your house. It won't cost you a dime in money, just equity in your house."

The couple looks at each other. "Why not? That's all we wanted the $4,000 for anyway."

Mike Dugan has the muscles and the brains, but there's just one more thing that he needs and he doesn't have—a truck.

But he doesn't let that stop him. He has loaded and unloaded trucks enough to know a few truck drivers who own their own rigs. He picks one out and starts talking to him.

"Tom, how'd you like to go partners with me on a little real estate venture? We'd share all the profits half and half."

"Are you kidding?" asks Tom. "In the first place, I know zilch about real estate, and I don't want to get involved in something I don't know anything about. In the second place, I don't have enough cash to keep my wife happy as it is. I sure don't have any extra to fool around with on real estate."

Mike grins. "Don't worry about it. It's not that hard. All you've got to do is supply your truck and your muscles." Mike Dugan has just made his first real estate deal.

54   The "Fixer-Upper" Partner

Mike Dugan continues to look for good deals in real estate. He looks at the HOUSE FOR SALE ads in the newspaper every day and goes out in person to check out the ones that seem the best. He makes a lot of offers and receives a lot of "No's" before he gets his share of the "Yes's."

He is out there finding good deals every week. One day, he comes across what looks like a really good buy. It is definitely a fixer-upper. This house looks like a total shambles. It needs paint on the outside, new shingles on the roof, and the porch is sagging in the middle. Ordinary house hunters would take one look at this wreck and drive away fast.

But Mike Dugan is no ordinary house hunter. He is a bargain hunter, and that makes all the difference.

He goes inside to talk to the owner. "How much are you asking for your house, Mr. Howard?" The seller looks discouraged. "Well, I think about $27,500. This is a three bedroom house with a partially finished basement. The other houses in this neighborhood look fairly nice. This is the only house that looks like it has been through a war.

Mike is sure that when this house is fixed up right, it will sell for at least $35,000, maybe $40,000. He says, "Do you have an assumable mortgage on the house, Mr. Howard?"

"Yes, I have a mortgage of $18,000 and it is assumable."

"That would give you an equity of $19,500. Are you willing to take monthly payments for your equity? I'll make you monthly payments of 1% per month on your equity. That would give you $195 a month."

Mr. Howard looks worried. "I guess I could take monthly payments like that . . . if, you'd be willing to give me about $3,000 down in cash."

Mike looks around the house. "Of course, this house is going to take some fixing up before I can rent or resell it. That's going to cost me a lot of cash. I don't think I can afford to pay you $3,000 down and still have enough cash to fix up the place."

"I know the house needs some fixing up," replies Mr. Howard, "but I'm giving you a real bargain on the price."

"That's true," admits Mike. "But maybe we can work something out. Maybe we can work out a deal where I call in my contractor and do $3,000 worth of improvements on the house, and you give me that $3,000 in credit as a down payment. You'd still be getting your price for the house, and I would have at least $3,000 equity of my own in the property from the repairs I'd be making. Do you see what I mean?"

"Yes, I see. I'd go along with a deal like that." Now Mike goes out to try to get a contractor to fix up the house. He has one problem. He doesn't have $3,000 cash lying around to pay a contractor for the necessary repairs.

He doesn't have the cash, but he does have a plan. He presents his plan to four contractors. They all tell him, "No."

Then he picks out a younger contractor, one who is just starting out in the business. He says, "Andy, how would you like some extra business?"

"What kind of business?" asks Andy.

"I'm a real estate buyer," explains Mike. "I intend to be buying a lot of fixer-uppers. They're always good bargains because they're in bad condition and need fixing up. The seller knows this, so he's willing to sell at a lower price. I'm going to get a contractor like you to come in and fix up these places so I can resell them at a profit."

Andy looks hopeful at this. "So you want me to come in and fix up the houses for you?"

"What I really want you to do," says Mike, "is to be a partner with me in real estate investing. I have a deal going right now where we can fix up the house and receive credit for the down payment. In return for your fixing up the house for me, I'm willing to give you a 50% interest in it. When the property is fixed up right, I know we can sell it at a good profit. You'll get 50% of that profit."

"Well, yes, I guess I could do that. Of course, I'd have to be using my own materials to fix up the house, and I wouldn't get any money back from them right away."

"But you would make a real profit when we resell that house," said Mike. "And if we like working with each other on this deal, there will be many more deals like this in the future. I'll take care of all the monthly payments on the houses, rent

them out sometimes, and I'll handle the reselling of the houses.
I find the houses and buy them, you fix them up, I resell them,
and we both share the profits 50/50. Does that sound like a good
deal for you?"

Andy nods his head enthusiastically. "Yes, it's a great deal!"

Partners In Marriage And Real Estate 55

Bruce and Anita Lawrence are real estate investment partners. They are also partners of another kind. They are married.
They have a very close relationship, both in their marriage and
in their real estate business. They have a special system which
works very well in opening doors to good deals.

This is the way it works. They advertise in the newspaper:
WE BUY HOUSES. They give their phone number at the end of
the ad. They get many calls from many different people who
have houses for sale. Some of these houses they will want to
buy; others they will not. It is important for them to screen out
the ones they are interested in from the ones they are not. The
ones they are interested in are ones which will give them good
terms in buying the property. They can find out most of this information over the phone, so that they do not go out wasting
their time looking at houses owned by people who are going to
demand all cash for their properties. But Bruce and Anita have
gone one step farther. Their technique helps to influence the
sellers to be more willing to give good terms on their properties.

Here is an example of a typical phone call they receive.

"Hello," comes a man's voice on the phone. "Are you the
one who advertised in the newspaper that you buy houses?"

"Yes, I'm Anita Lawrence. My husband and I work together
as partners in buying houses. Bruce isn't here right now, but

maybe I can talk to you and get some information down on paper. First of all, what is your name and phone number?"

"This is John Whitlock. My number is 555-9073."

"All right, Mr. Whitlock. Let me ask you a few questions, and I'll give the information to Bruce when he comes home." This approach gives Mr. Whitlock the secure feeling that Anita is on his side; she is going to present his information to Bruce, hoping that he will like it and go look at Mr. Whitlock's house.

"How much are you asking for your house, Mr. Whitlock?"

"$72,000."

"All right," says Anita. "Actually, this is a little higher price than Bruce is usually willing to pay for a house. I'll see what he says."

"Well, we might sell it for $70,000 if you wanted to buy it right away."

"That's good, but let me continue with a few more questions. Do you have an assumable loan, and if so, will it be assumable by another buyer if we resell the house?"

"Yes, our mortgage is assumable. It's $42,000."

"Then if Bruce does agree to buy your house at a price of $70,000, that would give you an equity of $28,000."

"Yes," says the seller. "And we'd like to get all cash for our equity."

"Uh oh," says Anita. "We may have run into a little snag. I don't think Bruce would ever be willing to pay that much cash down on a property. I'm going to ask you a question I know Bruce is going to want the answer to. Are you willing to carry a second mortgage on your equity? Bruce usually likes to pay monthly payments on the equity at 1% a month. That would give you monthly payments of $280."

"I'm not sure about that," says, Mr. Whitlock. "I don't know if I like the idea of monthly payments. We'd really like all our cash now."

"I'll have Bruce talk with you about these monthly payments. You know, monthly payments have some real good things going for them. If Bruce gives you the whole $28,000 right now in one large chunk, you'd have to pay taxes on the whole amount. This would force you into a higher tax bracket. You'd end up paying not only the taxes on the $28,000, but a higher tax rate on all your income for the entire year. If he is paying you $280 a month, you'll only have to declare what you actually receive each year. Remember, Bruce will be paying you interest on these monthly payments. By the time he is through paying off your $28,000 equity he'll actually be giving you three times that amount. He will really be paying you more like $84,000 for your equity instead of $28,000. Considering all I've said, do you think that you would be willing to take monthly payments for your equity?"

The seller answers slowly, "Well, we might be able to handle monthly payments, for most of the equity, anyway. But, we really do need $5,000 cash now."

Anita says, "All right, I'll tell Bruce that. So if Bruce is willing to give you $5,000 cash as down payment, then could you take the balance of your equity in monthly payments, at 1% a month?"

Mr. Whitlock says, "Yes, we'll certainly consider that."

Anita says, "One more thing, on this $5,000, do you really need it all right now? Could you take $2,000 of it now, and another $2,000 in six months, with the remaining $1,000 to be paid a year from now?"

Mr. Whitlock replies, "Well, I guess we could take just the first $2,000 now, but we would really need the other $3,000 three months from now."

"All right," says Anita. "I've written down all this information, and I'll give it to Bruce when he comes home. Hopefully, he will like this information. If he does, he'll be giving you a call this evening. Thank you for calling, Mr. Whitlock. I hope we'll be doing business with you."

Bruce and Anita use this technique all the time. Anita lets the owner of the house know that she is trying to get the deal accepted by her husband and partner, Bruce. If she can get a good enough deal, he'll be sure to accept it. Because of this, she is on the seller's side of the fence and can ask him open-ended questions. This technique works!

56   The Seller Can Be Your Partner

Mike Dugan has located a nice house on the west side of town. It is owned by the Lofgren family, and Mike can see that it is worth at least $60,000, fair market value. There is nothing at all wrong with this house; it is no fixer-upper. He knows this house would be easy to resell if he can get a good enough price on it.

He asks, "What is the best price you can give me on your house, Mr. Lofgren?"

Mr. Lofgren says, "Well, we've had it listed at $57,500. How does that sound to you?"

"It's a fair price," admits Mike. "It's just a little high for me. What is your mortgage amount now?"

"The mortgage is at $28,000."

"Would you be willing to take monthly payments on your equity?"

Mr. Lofgren pauses for a long moment. "We might. We would like a sizable down payment, though. Say, $6,000."

Mike does not have $6,000 cash, and even if he did, he would not want to bury it as a $6,000 down payment in a property. He thinks he will have to look up one of his partners and offer him a half interest in this house. At this point, that seems to be the only way he could buy the property.

Then he has another idea. "Mr. Lofgren, I am a real estate investor. I have partners who provide cash and credit to help me buy houses. In return, I give them a half interest in the properties I buy. I just had a thought here. How would you like to be my partner in buying your house?"

Mr. and Mrs. Lofgren look at each other in amazement. "What do you mean?"

"Just this: I would like you to lower the selling price to $55,000 and drop the down payment altogether. I'll take over your existing mortgage with the bank and start making regular monthly payments of 1% per month on your $17,000 equity. That will be $170 per month I'll be paying you. I'll give you one-half of the equity growth in this house from the time I purchase it from you. The house will continue to appreciate, and when I resell it, it will be at a profit. I'll share half this profit with you, plain and simple."

Mr. and Mrs. Lofgren look at each other, considering the offer. "All right, young man, we'll become your partners in buying our house."

57

No Cash, Higher Income Partners

Randy Jones finds a nice home for sale near where he lives. He talks with the people, a family named Sullivan. They want $60,000 for their house. He knows this is a fair price and asks them if they are willing to take monthly payments for their equity.

Mrs. Sullivan answers, "Are you willing to give us a $6,000 down payment, in cash?"

"Sure, if you'll let me buy your equity on monthly payments." Randy explains the terms of 1% per month, and the Sullivans agree.

As he leaves, Randy says, "I'm going to make arrangements for the $6,000 cash down payment. I'll be back tomorrow."

He decides to look for a successful businessman as his partner.

There is a new computer store in his area of town, and it seems to be doing very well. He drops in and asks to see the owner.

In a few moments, a young man comes out to talk to him. "Hi, I'm Cleave Jackson. You wanted to speak to me?"

"Yes," said Randy. "I have a business proposition for you. Tell me, do you know about the benefits of a real estate investment?"

"No, not exactly. But I'd be interested in hearing about them."

Randy proceeds to explain. When he has finished, he says, "I'm looking for a partner who has $6,000 to invest as a down payment in a nice property I've just found. I'd give you 100% of the depreciation and 50% of the appreciation. When I resell the house, you'll get 50% of the profits. Are you interested?"

"Yes, I am," says Cleave seriously. "There's just one catch. I don't have $6,000 in cash."

Randy is surprised. "Why, this looks like a very successful computer business you have going for you here."

"Yes, we have a good income from it, but I'm just starting out, and haven't built up any cash reserves yet. I just don't have $6,000 to invest in anything right now."

"Oh . . . " But Randy is thinking quickly. "So, you have no ready cash on hand, but you do have a high monthly income. Right?"

"Right."

"Then tell me this. Would you be willing to put out part of your monthly income on investment?"

"Yes, I'd be willing to do that, if I'd still get my half interest in the property."

Randy nods, "I'll see that you get it."

He discusses Cleave's monthly income with him, and determines how much of it can be used on this investment. Then he goes back and talks to the Sullivans. "I can't pay you your $6,000 cash all in one shot, but I can pay it in several smaller ones. I'll pay you your regular monthly installments on your equity and give you $250 a month over and above those monthly payments. I'll pay off your $6,000 down payment within three years."

The sellers consult with one another. Then Mr. Sullivan says, "Three years is a little too long for that. Could you possibly pay it off in one? If you do, we'll call it a deal."

Randy knows from talking with Cleave that he could afford to pay as much as $650 a month on an investment. And he knows that he can rent the house for more than enough to make the regular mortgage payments. He says, "All right, we'll pay you $500 a month above the regular mortgage payments, and then you'll have your full $6,000 in cash by the end of one year."

They agree, and the deal is made.

Sometimes a person has no ready cash in reserve, but does have a high monthly income and is willing to invest it a month at a time. These people should not be overlooked as partners in real estate investment.

58   Limited Partners

Mike Dugan has found a $50,000 house for sale in a nice neighborhood. The house is in excellent shape and would be ready to go on the market for immediate resale if the price is right. He looks the house over carefully and is sure he can sell it for at least $54,000. The owner agrees to take monthly payments for his equity if Mike will give him a down payment of $4,000 in cash. Mike agrees, but asks for two weeks to raise the money. The owner says yes.

Mike does not have any wealthy partner to finance this deal. He knows he has to do it some other way. He talks to his friends. None of them are wealthy, but all have some income and a little money put away in savings.

He presents his proposal. "My friends, I've got a good deal here. I've found a nice house for $50,000 and I know I can resell it for at least $54,000."

"That will be a $4,000 profit. I need $4,000 to make the down payment. If each one of you put up $1,000 that I can use for the down payment, I'll give each of you a 50% interest in the property. You'll get half the appreciation and half the profit when I resell the house. Each one of you who is investing $1,000 will get 1/4 of that 50% of the profit. Do you understand?"

They nod. "Yes," says one of them. "I can shell out $1,000 right now on a deal like this."

Another says, "Shouldn't we make this thing legal?"

"Yes," Mike agrees. "We need to go to an attorney and have him draw up a limited partnership." Business concluded, Mike collects the $1,000 from each of them, and takes the $4,000 to pay the owner his cash down payment.

He buys the house, rents it out for a few months, and eventually finds a buyer for it at $55,000.

He calls his friends together and gives them their 50% of the profit. One of them holds the check in his hand and says, "Mike, can you do that again?"

Mike assures him he can. "Then let's keep this "limited partnership" thing together. Mike's the real estate brain here, let him find the places and buy them. We'll all chip in for the down payment. This is a good way for us to get some extra cash."

Mike Dugan has successfully formed his limited partnership group. He knows the people he can call on for down payment money, and he can duplicate his success.

Discounting Underlying Notes For Cash 59

Randy Jones has found a house at a selling price of $62,000. He talks to the owners, Mr. and Mrs. Wilson, and they are willing to drop the price to $60,000. They have a $38,000 mortgage from a private party, Mr. Jorgenson.

Randy goes to Mr. Jorgenson's home to talk to him about assuming the mortgage. The seller says, "I'm not sure about this. If I let you assume this mortgage I want to be sure that you are going to be able to make all the monthly payments. Frankly, I've been worried sometimes that the Wilsons were not going to come through with that money every month. Sometimes they've been late with it. To tell you the truth, I'm getting kind of tired of being a mortgage holder."

Randy takes the hint. He has heard about cases like this. He knows that sometimes these people are willing to take big discounts for cash. So he says, "Maybe that can be arranged, Mr. Jorgenson. If I give you all cash for this mortgage, would you be willing to give me a discount on it? Say 50%?"

The seller shakes his head. "Not that much. But I would be willing to discount it at 65%."

"All right," says Randy. "That sounds like a good deal to me. Let me talk to my partner about this. I think I can have the money for you within two weeks."

They sign an agreement to this effect and Randy leaves. He goes to talk with Mr. VanFleet, the owner of the big department store where he works. "Mr. VanFleet, I have a deal here that I think you'll really like. We can buy a $38,000 first mortgage at a big discount. We would only have to pay 65% of the face value of $38,000." He takes out his pocket calculator. "We would have to pay $24,700 in cash for a $38,000 mortgage. That would be a profit of $13,300. If we resell the house, even if we resold it for the same price we're buying it for, we would have a built-in equity of $13,300. That would be solid profit."

Mr. VanFleet nods. "Good work, Randy. I'll buy that one."

Mr. VanFleet puts up the money, Mr. Jorgenson sells them the $38,000 mortgage at 65%, and Randy and Mr. VanFleet buy the Wilson's home.

Randy puts the place up for resale immediately. Within three weeks they have a buyer at $62,000. This is $2,000 over the price Randy paid for the house. This adds to the $13,300 equity they already have in the house from the discounted first mortgage. Randy and Mr. VanFleet receive a total profit of $15,300 on the resale of the property. They share this profit equally, according to their agreement.

This gives Randy a profit of $7,650 on the buying and re-selling of this house. $6,650 of this is the profit on the discounted mortgage.

When you buy and resell houses, discount mortgages are a very profitable business!

Section 7

Getting Them The Money Later

Getting Them
The Money Later

One of the great things about delaying payments and getting the money to the sellers six to twelve months after the sale date is that you have some room to make a really nice profit.

If you have six months to make your down payment, you could immediately sell the house at a profit or start renting it out and sell it as a rental. These are a couple of ways of making a profit before you are required to pay the down payment. See if the seller will work with you in this way, but make sure it benefits him too. You can do this by increasing the amount you pay him either on the down payment or on the price of the property. Let him make the choice of the options you suggest, as long as you can handle them too.

As Randy, our now experienced buyer, is finding out, there is more than one way to delay payments and still make money on a house free and clear. This gets more and more exciting with each new scenario.

Delayed
Down Payment

60

Randy Jones has found a $50,000 house in a nice neighborhood. The house is in good condition and he knows that he can get $50,000 for it on a resale. He talks with the owner. "What is the lowest price you could sell your house for, Mr. Wallace?"

Mr. Wallace considers. "I'd let it go at $47,500."

"Does it have an assumable mortgage?"

"Yes. The mortgage is worth $32,000."

"Will you take monthly payments for your equity?" Randy asks.

The seller looks at his wife for a moment, then replies "We'd be willing to do that if you could give us a down payment of $5,000."

Randy does not have $5,000 cash and Mr. VanFleet is out of town on a business trip. He has already concluded a deal this month with Esther and Irv, and knows they have used up most of their ready cash.

He tries something new. "All right, Mr. Wallace. I'll give you the $5,000 down payment. I can't give it to you right now, but I can give it to you in six months. If you like, I'll put that in writing and sign it in the presence of a lawyer."

"You'll give us the whole $5,000 in one lump sum at the end of six months?" asks Mr. Wallace.

"Right."

The Wallaces talk it over. Then Mr. Wallace says, "That sounds fair enough. However, you must start making payments on the equity right away. That has to be in the agreement."

Randy agrees. He goes to the closing without Mr. VanFleet or Esther or Irv as his partners. He signs the agreement, written up by the Wallace's lawyer, that he will pay the whole $5,000 down payment at the end of six months. If he does not, the Wallace's will have a right to foreclose on the house and take it back. Randy will lose all his mortgage payments over those six months.

The Wallaces feel secure, and Randy has gotten a good deal on this house. He takes possession, cleans it up a bit, mows the lawn, paints the fence and the front porch, and puts the house up for resale in two weeks at a price of $52,500. Less than a month later, a buyer offers him $51,000 for the place. Randy accepts. The new buyer assumes the first mortgage at the bank and the second mortgage with the Wallaces and gives Randy cash for his remaining equity.

The Wallaces sold the house to Randy at $47,500 with a $5,000 down payment. This gives him a $5,000 equity in the house at a price of $47,500. He is selling the house at $51,000, $3,500 above what he paid for it. At a selling price of $51,000, Randy will have an equity of $8,500.

He takes $5,000 of this money and pays the Wallaces their $5,000 down payment. This leaves him $3,500 profit.

By getting a delayed down payment and taking possession of the house, Randy was able to resell the property at a profit, use the money to pay the down payment, and have money left over for a profit.

61   Delayed Down Payment: Added Interest

Randy Jones is out looking for houses every day. He finds another single-family dwelling which he judges will sell at about $45,000. He tells Mr. Russell, the owner, "I can buy your house if you give me a good enough price. How low would you be willing to go for a quick sale right now?"

Mr. Russell looks at him and sees that he is dead serious. He thinks a minute and says, "My best price would be $41,000. That's as low as I could go."

Randy asks some more questions and finds out there is a $30,000 assumable mortgage on the house. "You have $11,000 in equity in this house. I'd like to pay you that equity on a second mortgage, giving you 1% per month."

Mr. Russell thinks about it and says, "I'll sell the house to you on those terms, if you can give me $3,000 cash for a down payment."

Randy has learned some things in dealing with sellers. "I'm willing to give you $3,000 in cash, but I'd like to give it to you a year from now." He always starts out by asking for a year.

Mr. Russell says, "A year is too long. How about six months?"

"I'll go along with six months," says Randy. He was willing to go along with six months in the first place. He always starts out at a year, so he will have something to bargain with.

Mr. Russell says, "I'm not willing to wait six months for my down payment unless I'm going to get some really good interest. Are you willing to give me interest on it?"

"Yes," says Randy. "I'll give you 10% interest."

"That's not enough. I'd like 20%."

"I'll tell you what I'll do ," says Randy, "I'll give you 17%. That's a good healthy interest rate."

Mr. Russell smiles. "All right, I'll settle for 17%." Randy buys the house on these terms and puts ads in the newspaper the same day he takes possession of the property. He advertises the house at $45,000. Eight days later a buyer offers him $44,000. He takes it.

Randy knows if he can delay his payment of cash into a property he is buying, he will have enough time to sell the house and get the cash he needs to pay the down payment. In effect, this is buying houses with no money down.

62 Delayed Down Payment: Increase Price Of House

Randy finds another house for sale. This one is a real buy. It needs some work, and the owner, Mr. Donaldson, is offering it for $38,000. When fixed up a little, it should be worth as much as the house he has just sold: $44,000. Randy says, "I'll buy it at that price if you'll let me pay monthly payments on your equity." Randy is getting to be an old pro at this game. No matter who he is talking with, he always asks to pay off the equity in monthly payments.

Mr. Donaldson hesitates. "I don't know. Well, I guess I could. However, I'd have to have $3,000 down in cash."

Now Randy asks the next question, one he has learned to ask well. "Are you willing to take that $3,000 a year from now?"

Again, Mr. Donaldson hesitates. "Tell me, why should I let you take a year to pay me what should be mine in the first place. That does you some good, but it sure doesn't do me any good."

"I see what you mean," says Randy. "If you let me give you monthly payments on your equity and let me pay you that $3,000, in say, six months instead of a year, I'll give you $39,000 for the house instead of $38,000. The mortgage on your equity will be $1,000 higher, because I'll be making higher monthly payments. That should do you some good."

Mr. Donaldson smiles. "Yes, it would. All right, I'll sell to you on those terms."

Randy takes possession of the house and fixes it up a little, at a cost of $800. In three weeks, he has the house on the market. In two weeks he has a buyer at $43,000. Randy thinks he could have sold the house at $45,000, but he can sell it for $43,000 now. He accepts the offer. Again, the delayed down payment has given him time to get the house ready, on the market, and sold, before he ever has to pay on the down payment. Raising his buying price on the home by $1,000 has been made up for by reselling the house quickly.

Delayed But Increased Down Payment   **63**

Randy is enjoying this game of delayed down payments. He is eager to try again. He knows that some people will give you a delayed down payment simply if you ask for it, while others need a little more convincing. Money, in one way or another, is what convinces them.

He finds another house for sale in good condition. It looks as though it would be worth $52,000. He is right; when he asks the owner's price, it is exactly $52,000. Randy goes to work. "This is a nice house, and I'd like to buy it. $52,000 is just more than I could pay you for it. Could you drop the price a little? Tell me the least you could take for it. If I can live with that price, I'll buy your house today."

Mr. Albertson says, "I suppose I could let it go at $48,000. But that's the lowest I'll go."

"I can buy it at that price if I can assume your mortgage and give you a second mortgage for your equity. I'll pay you 1% per month on that equity."

Mr. Albertson counters, "I'd be willing to do that, but I'd need a down payment of $3,000 cash, can you handle that?"

"I can handle it a little farther down the road, say a year from now."

Mr. Albertson replies, "How about six months?"

"Six months it is," says Randy.

"But," says Mr. Albertson, "I'm still not sure if I would want to go through with a deal like that. No, I don't think so. Why should I let you have six months to give me that $3,000?"

"Because at the end of that six months I'll give you $4,000 instead of $3,000."

"Oh . . . " Mr. Albertson is really thinking it over now. "Yes, that sounds like a decent trade-off. You give me $4,000 at the end of six months instead of $3,000 now. Okay, it's a deal."

Randy is learning how to buy time with money—money which he will pay in some form or other at a later date. He is giving these sellers down payments in cash on their houses when he has gotten his cash from a quick resale. Again, he is buying these properties with no money down.

64 Mortgage Due In Six Months: All Cash

Randy has now found a single-family home with a fair market value of $55,000. He talks with the owners, Mr. and Mrs. Bradley.

"Mr. Bradley, what is the best price you could give me on your house, I mean, the lowest price you would accept and still feel happy with?"

The Bradleys talk it over between themselves for a while and finally say, "We would settle for a price of $52,000."

"Would you be willing to take monthly payments on your equity?"

Again, the Bradleys talk it over between the two of them. "I'm afraid not. I think we're going to have to have all cash for our house at this price."

Randy thinks about it. "All right, I'll tell you what I'll do. I'll sign an agreement to pay you the full $52,000 in cash within one year. If you like, we can go to a lawyer and have it drawn up legally."

Mr. Bradley agrees, "But, could you make that six months instead of one year?"

"All right," says Randy. He is sure he can resell this house at a profit before the six months are up. He is getting a good deal on the house, so he can give a good deal to the next buyer.

Randy Jones and the Bradleys go to a lawyer the next day and draw up the agreement. They go through closing, and Randy purchases the house. He has paid nothing down. Six months from now his mortgage of $52,000 is due in full. If he does not pay it, he will lose the house.

He takes possession of the house and immediately puts it up for resale at a price of $55,000. Two weeks later a family comes along and pays him the full $55,000 he is asking for the house. He takes this money, uses $52,000 of it to pay off the Bradleys and has $3,000 in profit left over.

65 Mortgage Due In One Payment In Six Months: Offer Higher Price

Randy likes to deal with single-family houses. There are more of them on the market and more people looking for them than any other kind of property. This makes them easy to resell. Today he has found another one, simply by reading the newspapers. He reads the HOUSES FOR SALE section in the classified ads every day.

He is out looking at this house right now, and talking with the owner, Mr. Harshaw. "How much are you asking for your home, Mr. Harshaw?"

"$59,000," replies Mr. Harshaw. "$37,000 of that is a mortgage with the bank. You can assume that. I've checked."

"Would you be willing to sell at a price of $55,000?" Mr. Harshaw shakes his head slowly. "No, I wouldn't. $59,000 is the price."

"Are you willing to take monthly payments on your equity?"

Mr. Harshaw purses his lips, "Yes, but I'd have to have a $5,000 down payment."

This is a really nice home. It's in a nice neighborhood, and $59,000 is really a low price for it. In fact, this house is a bargain. Randy decides to go all out for a resale. He says, "What do you say we forget all about the monthly payments, also the down payments? Suppose I just give you the $59,000 all in cash, all in one shot? I'll buy the house from you right now at that price. In the purchase agreement I'll agree to pay you the total of $59,000 one year from now."

Mr. Harshaw almost likes this arrangement, however, he doesn't seem to like it quite enough. He says, "I like having the cash, but I'd like it in six months instead of a year."

Randy decides to sweeten the pot a little. He says, "You could sell it to someone else for $59,500 right now. But six months from now, I'll pay you $64,000 for the house. And I'll put that in writing."

"Well," says Mr. Harshaw. "That does make it sound a lot better. Okay. Let's go to my lawyer in the morning, and we'll write up the agreement."

This is a really nice house. Randy buys it, takes possession, and rents it to a nice family. Since he is not making any payments on the house for six months, he is able to collect the rent on the house as pure profit. After collecting rent for four months, he puts the house up for sale at $70,000. Three weeks later he accepts an offer of $67,000. He pays Mr. Harshaw the $64,000 due in the delayed one payment mortgage note, and has $4,000 cash left over, plus the $600 a month he has been collecting in rent every month.

He has learned his lesson very well. When you own a property and you are not making any payments on it of any kind, you have room to make some really nice profit.

Delayed Regular Mortgage: Raise Price Of House   **66**

Randy Jones is really succeeding with this new idea of getting the money to the seller later. He has been successful in two areas: delaying the down payment, and giving the seller a delayed mortgage due in full at the end of six months. He has been thinking about these techniques, and now he is ready to try a new one. Today he has found another house that looks good. He talks with the seller about it.

"How much are you asking for your home, Mr. Marner?"

"$55,000. I have a $38,000 mortgage on it, which is assumable."

Randy does not quibble about this price. He knows it is a reasonable price for this house, and that he can resell the house later at a price of $60,000. If he buys the house at $55,000 he knows that he can always come down from his $60,000 price to something like $58,000 for a quick resale.

He says, "Will you take monthly payments on your equity? If so, I'll make you payments of 1% per month."

Mr. Marner seems surprised at first, but then says, "That might be possible." Randy is looking for time he can use in reselling the house. He says, "I need a little time here. I'd like to hold off on making any payments to you for at least six months. Then I'll start making the payments to you regularly."

Mr. Marner crinkles up his brow a little. "Now, wait a minute. I don't know about that part of it. I'd rather have the money coming in right away."

"Yes, I can understand that," says Randy. He knows he has to "sweeten the pot" a little for Mr. Marner, so he says, "I'll tell you what I'll do, Mr. Marner, you let me wait six months to start making you these payments, and instead of giving you $55,000 for the house, I'll give you $57,000."

This makes a real difference to Mr. Marner. That's $2,000 more for his house. "Yes, that sounds much better to me. Yes, if you'll give me $57,000 for the house, I'll hold off on your payments for six months."

Randy buys the house on these terms, and rents it out for four months, collecting the rent every month and not having to make any payments to Mr. Marner during this time. Then he puts the house up for resale at $62,000 and accepts an offer from a buyer at $59,000.

He makes $2,000 profit on the resale of the house, plus the $550 per month rent from the tenants.

Randy knows that any time he can delay the payment of any of his money for a house, it gives him time to make some money on that house free and clear. It also gives him a chance to resell the house and get the money he needs to pay the seller.

Delayed Regular Mortgage: High Interest **67**

Randy Jones has another idea this time. It worked very well before, giving the seller of the house a higher price for his home in exchange for delaying regular monthly payments on the equity. Now he has thought of a new angle and is eager to try it.

The next house he finds is another single-family dwelling, Randy's favorite for buying and reselling. It is in fairly good condition, but could stand a little work, probably about $1,000 worth to put it in top-notch condition. He talks to the owner, Mr. Klein. "You have a good house here, Mr. Klein. It could stand a little work, though. I'll probably have to put about $1,000 into it before I can put it up for resale. Considering that, what would be the least you could possibly take for it and still feel comfortable?"

Mr. Klein considers. "I know it needs a little work, maybe not $1,000 worth, but it does need some. I'd let the house go at a price of $48,000."

Randy estimates he could resell this house at a price of $55,000 if it was fixed up right. "All right, $48,000 seems about right for this place. I'll give you that much for it if you will do two things for me. First, I'd like to pay off your equity by giving you regular monthly payments at 1% per month. I'd be paying you 10% interest, so you'd end up with about three times as much profit in the long run."

Mr. Klein raises his eyebrows. "I'd be willing to take monthly payments for my equity. What is the second thing?"

"The second is this. I'm going to need some time to really fix your place up nice so I can resell it. I'd like to delay starting my monthly payments to you for at least six months. That will give me time to fix it up right."

Mr. Klein answers, "What benefit is there in this for me if I let you delay your payments for six months?"

"Just this," says Randy. "If you let me delay my payments for six months, I'll give you 11% interest on your equity instead of 10%. That way you'll end up with even more money in the long run."

This makes the point. Randy is really making money on this delayed mortgage business. The seller is getting his money out of it, even if it is delayed for a while, and Randy is buying his houses with no down payments!

68 Delayed Down Payment And Delayed Mortgage: Higher Price, Higher Interest

Randy Jones has found a tougher customer this time—that is, a tougher seller. The house for sale is in fine condition, and the owner knows it. When Randy asks him the least amount of money he would sell his house for, he replies, "$55,000, and not a bit less. It has an assumable mortgage on it of $42,000. I have an equity of $13,000. I want to be sure I get paid for my equity before I ever sell this place. Before we go any further, I want you to understand that."

"I read you loud and clear," says Randy. "I'll pay you for your equity. I'll even pay you extra for your equity if you will let me pay it off in monthly payments. I'll give you 1% per month on your equity, which will be $130 a month and I'll give you 9% interest on the equity. You'll end up getting three times as much money when you add up all the interest."

"That's true," says Mr. Gossertt. "That interest would bring a lot more money in the long run. All right, I'll go along with that if you'll give me a $3,000 down payment in cash in the beginning."

"I can give you the $3,000 down payment in cash," says Randy, "if you'll let me give it to you six months from now, and let me begin my regular monthly payments to you on your equity at that time also."

The seller frowns a little. "I don't like that part of it," he says. "I'd be losing money on my interest through those six months. I wouldn't be getting any interest at all."

Randy sees that Mr. Gossertt is a seller who needs some extra convincing. So he puts it all on the line in one shot. "Let's do it this way, then. You let me hold off for six months on giving you the down payment and the monthly payments, and I'll give you some extra interest. I'll give you 10% interest instead of 9%." He looks at Mr. Gossertt and sees that he is halfway convinced. So he adds, "And I'll even do this. I'll give you $2,000 extra on the selling price of your house. That will raise your equity another $2,000 and give you more interest in the long run."

This combination convinces Mr. Gossertt. "Yes, that makes it a better deal for me. Let's go ahead."

Randy knows that even though he is raising the price of the house along with the interest rate, it is still a good enough price for this property. He will be able to resell the house later at a profit, before the six months are up. This is important. He buys the house not only with no down payment, but no monthly payments to the seller in the beginning. He resells the house before he has to come up with the cash for the down payment. He not only has the money for the down payment, but the full resale price of the house in his pocket. He then has enough money to pay the down payment to the seller in full.

69   Moratorium On Interest Payments

Steve Wilson has found a property for sale. It is a four-plex and needs a little work. Two of the units are rentable, and are presently occupied. The other two units need some fixing up before they could be rented. Steve is negotiating with the owner on terms and price. Mr. Moran says, "I've got to have $125,000 for the place. It's a bargain at that price."

Steve can see that the four-plex is a bargain. He knows that Mr. Moran is giving him a good price on it because of the units that need repair. He says, "I'll pay $125,000 for your place, if you'll let me pay your equity in monthly installments. How much equity do you have here?"

"I have a mortgage of $86,000. At a selling price of $125,000, that gives me an equity of $39,000. As for taking monthly payments on my equity, let me ask you, would you be willing to pay interest on that?"

"Yes."

The seller nods. "I'll go ahead with the deal as long as you give me 10% interest on my equity."

Steve takes out his calculator and goes to work. He figures the income from the two rental units which are in working order, the monthly payments to the bank on the first mortgage, and the monthly payments he will be making to Mr. Moran for his equity. It comes out short. His calculations show clearly that at this time the property will generate only enough money to allow him to pay 6% interest to Mr. Moran on his equity. He puzzles over this for a little while. He finally says, "It just doesn't work, Mr. Moran. With only two units in condition to be rented now, I wouldn't be making enough money to pay you the full 10% interest. However, would you let me pay the monthly payments with no interest for the first year? That would give me time to fix up these two units. Then I'll have more income coming in from the property."

"That won't take a year," says Mr. Moran. "You should have those units ready in six months at the very latest. If you can't pay me all the interest during that time, I'd still like to have some of it."

Steve refigures. He sees that the property will be generating enough income to allow him to pay 6% interest on his payments to Mr. Moran. This will still allow him enough money to get the two other units in condition to rent. He says, "The most interest I could possibly pay you now is 6%. At the end of six months, I should be getting more income from the property and can give you the full 10%."

"Then I would be losing 4% interest over those six months."

Steve replies, "I'll see to it that you don't lose that 4% interest. We'll refigure the amount and I'll pay the total back to you by the end of the six months."

Mr. Moran is still not convinced. So Steve adds, "All right, then. I'll even do this. At the end of six months I'll give you 5% instead of 4%."

That extra interest does the trick. "That's good enough. You've just bought yourself a four-plex."

If you ever find yourself in this position, be sure to give your lowest offer first, then, walk your way up step by step until the seller is ready to accept your offer. In this case, Steve Wilson has enough time to fix up the rental units so that he will be bringing in the money he needs when he has to start paying that higher interest rate, plus a lot left over for profit.

70   One Great Deal Turned Into Three Terrific Deals!

Here is a great example which really illustrates this point. If this story had not happened to me personally, I would not believe it. Right outside of Tacoma, Washington, there was a small house for sale. A deal had just fallen through, so the people really wanted to sell the house quickly.

I went out and looked at this house. What a wreck! The paint was peeling off the walls! Besides that, it rains a lot in Tacoma and the home had a big beautiful layer of green moss two inches thick growing on the roof! It was a sad looking house, to be sure.

Did I walk away from the deal then? I could have said, "There's no way I'm going to be caught buying a dilapidated wreck like that!" But I didn't. I looked carefully at the whole picture.

The house was in a nice neighborhood. Its mature trees and shrubs gave the setting a pleasant atmosphere. Usually, when a house is in a nice neighborhood with nice surroundings, there is real hope for it, even if the house itself is a wreck.

I asked the lady who was selling the house, "How much are you asking for your home?"

She said, "$27,000." $27,000! I was really excited! Even if the house was a total wreck, this was a great price. I knew at $27,000 I could afford to fix the place up and sell it for a handsome profit.

Then the lady shattered my plans by adding, "I've got to have $7,000 cash!" Although the price was right, the terms were wrong.

I began talking with the lady, to find out her real reasons for wanting $7,000 down on a $27,000 house.

There were agents on my side and agents on her side. We all sat down together and talked. I love doing that. It drove the real estate agents crazy! They were all sitting there and everybody was afraid of what was going to happen. I was sitting calmly writing up the offers. I was doing what the real estate agents were supposed to be doing, writing up the offers while they were sitting back waiting for their commissions.

I said to the lady, "All right, $27,000 is a fair price for your house. But the down payment you are asking for is just too much. Do you really need that $7,000 all at once, right now?"

"Well," she said, "I'm going to have to pay that real estate agent his commission, and I'm also going to have to pay the closing costs on the sale of the house. That will come to at least $2,000."

"That sounds about right," I said. "You're going to need $2,000 now for the commission and the closing costs. But what about the other $5,000? What do you need it for? Do you really need that other $5,000 right now?"

This was a rental property and this lady absolutely hated it! She lived about 30 miles away, and this particular property had been vacant for six months. All she wanted was to get rid of it.

I knew that she was a classic case of the "Don't Wanter," and that if I made her an offer she could live with at all, she would take it.

When I asked her what she wanted that other $5,000 for, she said, "I need that other $5,000 to buy a dog kennel."

I just sat there looking at her. She was going to take that $5,000 and buy a dog kennel? She wanted to trade tenants for dogs? I said, "Well, that sounds great. When do you need the $5,000 to buy the dog kennel?"

She replied, "We're going to buy it in January, so I will need the money in December."

I said, "Great! This is May, that gives you plenty of time before December. How about this? I'll give you the $2,000 down right now, and that will take care of the real estate agent's commission and your closing costs. Then I'll sign a note to give you the other $5,000 on December 15th. That will give you your $5,000 in plenty of time to buy your dog kennel in January. How will that be?"

That was just fine. The lady loved the deal. She was getting rid of the property she hated, and getting the dog kennel she really wanted. These were the two things she wanted most in this deal. She got them both. Where do the three terrific deals come in? Well, there is more, much more, to this story! The following serves as a perfect illustration of still another technique, the technique of deferring monthly payments until a later date.

The lady was happy with my offer of $2,000 cash down, and the other $5,000 in December. The total selling price of the property was $27,000. $2,000 down plus $5,000 later left $20,000 for me to pay on the house. She still owed $7,000 on a loan from the bank. This left her $13,000 worth of equity in the property. The payments on her $7,000 loan at the bank were $250 a month at 8½% interest. The loan was assumable.

Then I started figuring. I realized that I could not pay off the $7,000 loan from the bank at $250 a month and at the same time make monthly payments to the lady on the $13,000.

This is something you must always watch for when you are buying property. Sometimes the bottom loans on the houses you are buying, the loans that are payable to the banks, have rather high monthly payments. In order to balance this out, you have to get low monthly payments on the loans you are creating from the seller. I said this to the lady, "The payment on the loan to the bank is too high. $250 monthly payment on $7,000 is way out of line. I won't be able to make any monthly payments on your $13,000 loan to me until I get this other loan paid off."

She said, "What are you talking about?" I went on to explain. "As soon as I finish paying off this $7,000 loan to the bank, 30 days later I will start making payments on your $13,000 loan, giving you $200 per month at 9% interest." She understood what I was talking about then, and said, "Oh, okay, I can handle that."

I thought that the loan to the bank would take about five or six years to pay off. Sure enough, when I checked it out, the $7,000 loan was going to pay off at the end of six years, that automatically clicked in my $13,000 loan from the seller and then this loan started paying off. That was it. That was all that I said in the agreement.

She loved this deal! She was glad to have her property unloaded, and have the money she needed to buy her dog kennel. That was all she wanted out of life at this point. She wanted that dog kennel so much that she was willing to let $13,000 of her money lie dormant in equity for six years, until that bottom loan to the bank was paid off.

The deal went through and I took possession of the property. Then the bombshell came! Three days later, the lady down at the escrow company called me on the phone, and she said, "Wade, what are you going to do with those houses out there?"

I said, "What do you mean 'houses out there'?" She said, "You bought three houses." I was bewildered. I said, "No, I didn't. I just bought the one house on Portland Avenue."

She said, "No, Wade, you ought to read the legal description. There is a total of three houses out there."

I exclaimed, "You are kidding!" I went hustling out there in my car. Sure enough, I measured the whole thing off, and there were three houses on my new property! There were two two-bedroom houses, and a one bedroom house on the back part of the lot.

I had just bought three houses for $27,000 and I hadn't even known it! I was so excited I couldn't sleep for two nights!

71   Lump Sum In The Future

One of the easiest ways to successfully buy a property is to give the seller exactly what he wants (or close to it), but give it to him later!

Suppose you find a property with a fair market value of $60,000. The owner has an existing $50,000 first mortgage on the property, and $10,000 worth of equity. He wants this $10,000 in cash.

You sit down at the negotiation table and start talking. Tell him something like this: "You have a nice place here, Mr. Jones. I can see that it's worth $60,000. That's a fair price. I'm willing to give you the whole $60,000 that you're asking. I can take over your loan at the bank now and start making the monthly payments this month. That will leave the $10,000 I'll owe you for your equity. I don't have $10,000 right now, but I will pay you the full $10,000 plus interest on a note, secured by a second mortgage on your property here. I'd like to make the note payable in full 10 years from now."

Obviously, the longer you can set up this loan, the better. Ask for 10 years, and say nothing about the interest. Wait and see what he says next.

At this point, Mr. Jones might say something like this. "Ten years! Ten years is a long time. I can't wait that long without getting some money on the property. And what about interest? Are you willing to pay some interest on that $10,000?"

You say, "Yes, I'll pay 9% interest per annum."

Mr. Jones says, "And I'd like five years a lot better than ten. Could you pay it off in five years?"

You say, "All right. Let's make it five years. I'll pay the whole $10,000, plus interest, all in one lump sum at the end of five years."

Mr. Jones says, "That's pretty good, but I'd like to have some interest on the $10,000 every year?"

You say, "Okay. I'll pay the interest on it every year."

Mr. Jones says, "All right. I'll go along with that." Let's sit down and make out the papers together.

Start by offering him the lowest interest you would like, and if he says, "No, that's not enough. I want 10%, not 9%," then say, "All right. I'll pay you 10%." Always start low, and then if he wants to raise it a little, go ahead and raise it to the point where you both feel comfortable. He might even agree to the lump sum paid off in five or ten years and just let the interest accrue.

Whatever happens, the property has probably gone up in value much more than the loan. You get the growth on the property in appreciation. The seller gets only the interest on his loan to you. How else do you benefit? Your payments are lower now. You have only two payments to make—one to the bank on that first mortgage loan, and your yearly interest payments to the seller.

If you are going to give someone a balloon payment at the end of a certain time period, there will be a trade-off. The seller must give you either no payments at all or very low payments during the course of his loan to you.

Section 8

Other Ways Of Getting Them The Money

Other Ways Of Getting Them The Money

Is your net worth in the form of highly valued assets like houses, boats, or cars? It could be that you only own a few items such as furniture and appliances. Have you ever thought about using these as your down payment?

Often a seller will need extra cash for moving. He will figure out the cost to move his furniture and then give you that amount, or more, as the amount he wants for a down payment. If you find out that the down payment is for the move, ask him if he would be able to leave most or all of the furniture. Then he doesn't have to be concerned about spending that money on moving and can buy new furniture instead after he moves. Be careful though—some furniture can be of sentimental value to the owners, and you need to be sensitive about that.

One other thing to keep in mind about putting furniture or other assets into an agreement is that it's a good choice for you to suggest that the seller's attorney, not you, put this phrasing into the agreement. Your seller will be much more at ease with the sale if you do this.

Using bonds as a source for a down payment works well too. If a seller wants $10,000 in cash, ask him if he will accept bonds. For this, you will likely only have to pay $5,000. When the bonds mature, they will be worth the full $10,000. One of the scenarios in this section is similar to this idea.

Another scenario talks about sweat equity as all or part of the down payment. Sweat equity is the work you put into a house to fix it up. It includes the cost of the materials, time, and labor of a person, usually the buyer. Your time and labor are worth a lot. If you have the necessary skills, and the seller accepts, you can fix a house up as the down payment, and you get to reap the benefits of your hard work when you make a profit from selling the house!

Using Furniture And Appliances For Down Payment

72

Mike Dugan has found another nice house he wants to buy. It is located out at the west edge of town in a nice neighborhood. The owner, Mr. Myers, is showing him the home. Everything looks in good condition. Mike has been chatting with Mr. Myers, just being friendly and finding out everything he can about the situation. He says, "This is a pretty nice house. Where are you going to move after you sell, Mr. Myers?"

"We're moving to Cincinnati. I've got a good job waiting for me."

Mike nods. "Yeah, a good job is always a good reason to move. I've seen a lot of people move for that reason." He continues to look around the house. "What's the lowest price you could take for your home?"

Mr. Myers thinks it over for a little while. Then he says, "Well, it was appraised at $54,500. But I'd let you have it at $52,000 even. Is that enough of a break for you?"

"Yes, I guess it is. I've got another question for you. Would you let me pay you monthly payments on your equity?"

Mr. Myers is still feeling good, thinking about the job waiting for him in Cincinnati. "Yes, I'd even be willing to give you a break on that, provided we can come to an agreement on the terms. How much would you be willing to pay me per month for my equity?"

"I'd pay you 1% per month and 10% interest. I always try to be fair, and I think that's a fair deal between a buyer and a seller."

Mr. Myers smiles, "10% interest and 1% per month payments would be fine. However, I would like to get a down payment in the beginning."

"How much of a down payment would you need?" asks Mike.

"$3,000 would be fine," says Mr. Myers. Mike starts thinking about how he could come up with $3,000 to make this down payment. He always has his friends in his limited partnership he can fall back on for a down payment, but prefers to figure out a way to do this on his own. 50% of the profit is great, but 100% of the profit is even greater.

He says, "$3,000 down does sound fair, but it's also a lot of money for me right now. I hope you don't think I'm being nosy, but would you mind telling me what you're going to use that $3,000 for?"

Mr. Myers laughs. "No, not at all. Cincinnati is a long way from here, and we're going to need some extra money to move all this furniture."

Mike looks around at the furniture, and suddenly he has an idea. He says, "Suppose you didn't have to move all this furniture. Suppose you just left some of it here. You've got a good job waiting for you in Cincinnati, and you can buy new furniture when you get there. That would save the cost of moving this older furniture. Unless, of course, this furniture is a keepsake."

"That's a thought," says Mr. Myers.

"How about this then?" says Mike "You leave the older furniture behind that doesn't have any sentimental value, including the refrigerator, lawn mower, and some of that extra stuff in the garage, and I'll sign an agreement to get you your $3,000 cash within two months after I take possession of the house. I'll actually try and give you your money quicker than that, probably within a month or a couple of weeks. But I'd like two months leeway just to be sure. We can put it all in writing and if you like, your lawyer can write it up."

"That sounds fine to me, Mike, but I'd better go ask my wife about this last part. I'll see if she has sentimental attachment to any of the furniture." Mr. Myers goes back into the other end of the house to talk alone with his wife. After 10 minutes or so he comes back. "It's all settled. We'll leave the furniture here."

Mike buys the house, and takes possession of it without actually having paid any cash as a down payment.

Now he has two months to come up with the $3,000 cash. He wants to do this by selling the furniture and other items that the Myers have left behind. He can either go to a dealer for this and sell the material to him wholesale, or he can try to sell the items separately to individuals. He decides to try selling to private individuals first, because they will be buying at retail instead of wholesale prices.

Mike cleans up the house and the yard and has a big garage sale. He advertises in the local newspaper, puts a big sign in the yard, and puts up notices on all the bulletin boards in this part of town, in grocery stores, laundromats, and anywhere else he can think of.

He has a big turnout for the garage sale and sells all the furniture, all the items left in the garage, and even the freezer and refrigerator left in the house. All this brings in a little over $3,400 in cash. He sends a check for $3,000 to the Myers, and he has a little over $400 profit left over. He has bought a nice house using none of his own cash as down payment.

Selling Off Part Of The Property To Raise The Down Payment Money

73

Mike Dugan is becoming more active as a real estate investor. He reads the ads in the newspaper every day and makes a lot of calls. He goes to see a lot of these places. He makes offers and some of his offers are accepted.

Today he thinks he has found another winner, a nice house at the northwest edge of town with rural country beyond. There is a large lot with the house. The house itself is in good condition and the owner is showing Mike through the house. Everything looks okay to him, so he asks, "How much are you asking for your house, Mr. Cartwright?"

Mr. Cartwright says, "$60,000. I think it's really worth a little more than that, but we'll settle for $60,000."

"That seems like a fair price for this place," says Mike. From what he has experienced with buying and selling houses, Mike is sure that he can sell this house for at least $65,000. He asks, "How much equity do you have and would you be willing to take monthly payments on it?"

The seller thinks about this. "Well, I guess I'd be willing to take monthly payments on it if I received a good healthy down payment. I'd like about $6,000 down, in cash."

"$6,000 in cash!" Mike's mind begins to work. The furniture deal worked very well last time, so he decides to try it again. The furniture in this home will not cover the whole down payment but should be worth about $2,000. He says, "If I pay you that $6,000 in cash, could you perhaps leave some of your furniture here when you move? And do you have some things in the garage you won't be taking?"

"I guess we could leave some of it for you." Mike knows this will not be nearly enough. He says, "I'm going to need a little time to raise the $6,000 cash. But I'll write into the purchase agreement that I will pay you that $6,000 within six months of the closing date. I'll really try to get the money to you long before that. You can have your lawyer draw it up."

Mike is learning to let the seller's lawyer write these clauses into the contract to put the seller's mind at ease.

"How much land comes with this house, Mr. Cartwright?"

"About four acres. It goes on down the road until you reach that fence right there, and then goes back to those trees. It's a good-sized lot."

This gives Mike another idea. He proceeds to city hall to find out if this property can be subdivided. The lady at city hall tells him that the property can indeed be subdivided.

Mike goes ahead and buys the house and immediately splits the land up into two extra lots and puts them up for sale. One lot sells for $4,000, and the other sells for $6,000. He uses $6,000 of this to pay off Mr. Cartwright for his down payment, and has a profit left over of $4,000.

He has just bought a house for no money down, and without even selling the house again he has made a profit of $4,000 on it!

Rental Deposits, Rent, & Real Estate Credits As Down Payments 74-76

Randy Jones has found a real buy this time. It is a 10-unit apartment building. The university is on one side and a big shopping center is on the other side. Every unit is presently rented; he has made sure of that. The tenants seem happy living there. This is a good sign. As he looks the place over, he realizes that he would not mind living here himself. This gives him some great ideas.

He talks with Mr. Adams, the owner. "I'd like to buy your apartment building, Mr. Adams, if I can handle the price and the terms. What's the lowest price you could give me on this building?"

Mr. Adams thinks a moment. "$200,000. That's $20,000 for each unit."

Randy nods. "They're well worth it." Then he asks the question he asks every seller: "Are you willing to let me pay you monthly payments on your equity? I'll pay you 1% per month on the equity and give you an added 9% interest."

There is a long silence from Mr. Adams. Randy continues, "If I pay you these monthly payments at interest, you'll end up with about three times as much money in the long run. And, you'd be taking it off your taxes one year at a time instead of all at once."

Both of these strike home. Mr. Adams responds slowly, "Yes, I can see the advantages of that arrangement. Yes, I'd accept monthly payments on my equity. But I've got to have a sizable down payment in the beginning, like $10,000 in cash."

"It's a deal," says Randy. He knows he can get this much cash from Mr. VanFleet if he brings him into this deal as a partner. Randy would be very happy with this arrangement. He would own half of a 10 unit apartment building and get half the income from the rentals, or maybe even more if Mr. VanFleet is feeling generous.

He does not feel like telling Mr. VanFleet about this deal just yet. He wants to see if he can come up with $10,000 cash in some other way. If he can do this, then he will own 100% of this 10 unit apartment building. 100% is better than 50%. He asks Mr. Adams to let him see all the facts and figures pertaining to the property. The first thing he looks into is the rental deposit fund. He finds out that each renter has paid a $400 security deposit upon moving into the apartment building. This is held in a separate fund. All this money will become his when he buys the apartment building. He does not need his pocket calculator to tell him that $400 per unit times 10 units equals a total of $4,000! He is really excited about this. This will amount to almost half his cash down payment.

Randy now has $4,000 out of the $10,000 he needs for a down payment on this 10 unit apartment building. The rental deposits will take care of the first $4,000. He needs $6,000 more.

He continues to search. He goes into the legal papers on the apartment building and reads about this escrow account. This is the account which holds money set aside to be used during the course of the year to pay the taxes month by month. He takes all these papers to a lawyer and asks him, "What's the story on this escrow account? What happens when someone comes along and buys this apartment building?"

Mr. Sims, the lawyer, says to him, "All that money in the escrow account goes to the new owner of the building. It's supposed to stay in that account until it is used to pay the taxes every month."

"But all that money does become the property of the new buyer as soon as he buys the building, right?"

The lawyer nods. "That's right. But you can't take it out of the account for anything except paying the taxes."

Randy thinks about this. "Then do you mean that if I buy this property, even if I can't spend this money for anything but the taxes every month, the money is actually mine?"

"Yes," Mr. Sims assures him.

"Then could I use the money in this account and declare it as a credit, as part of the down payment when I buy the apartment building?"

"That's right. You can do this legally. Write it as a cash credit on your purchase agreement and bring it to me when you're ready and I'll write it up for you." Randy looks into the figures. There is just over $5,200 in this account! He can use this $5,200 as credit on his down payment when he buys the apartment building! This $5,200 plus the $4,000 cash in the rental deposits add up to $9,200. Randy feels assured that he is going to make this $10,000 down payment on his own, without Mr. VanFleet as his partner.

Randy Jones now has $9,200 cash credit out of the $10,000 total he needs for a down payment on this 10 unit apartment building. He has only $800 left to go on this. He continues to search through the legal papers on the property and think about the situation.

The rent on each apartment unit is $400 per month. Ten units time $400 a month equals $4,000. All this money is due from the tenants on the first of every month. That makes $4,000 coming in on the first of every month.

This $4,000 would more than finish up the $10,000 he needs. But he will have to make his mortgage payment to Mr. Adams on the first of every month. Therefore, he will not have nearly all of this $10,000 to pay as a down payment on the property. He thinks about it some more. He suddenly has what he thinks is a brilliant idea. He takes off for the lawyer's office to check with him. "Mr. Sims," he says. "I want to ask you another question. If I buy this apartment building on the first of the month, and we have the closing on that date, who will get the rent on that day, the former owner or me? The rent is due on the first of every month."

"In this case, the new owner is the one who will receive all rents."

"And the mortgage payments," says Randy, "do I have to pay Mr. Adams that first mortgage payment on the day I buy the place from him, or on the first of the next month?"

"Your mortgage payments to him won't be due until the first of the month after you buy the building."

"That's all I needed to know!" exclaims Randy. He proceeds to set everything up so that the closing date comes on the first of the month. With Mr. Sims' help, he writes into the agreement that he is getting $4,000 credit for the rental deposits,

$5,200 for the real estate tax credits, and that he is entitled to receive the $4,000 in rent money from the tenants of the building. All of this ads up to $13,200.

In this way, Randy is able to come up with his $10,000 cash down payment, and, he still has $3,200 left over! He has just bought a $200,000 ten unit apartment building with none of his own cash down. He has even ended up with $3,200 in his pocket!

Refurbishing Fees 77

Mike Dugan has found another buy. This one is a fixer-upper. As he goes through the property, Mr. Beardall, the owner, says, "I can see that the place needs some fixing up, but it's basically in good condition. Wouldn't you agree?"

"Yes," says Mike. "It is going to cost something to fix it up though." He stops suddenly and looks at Mr. Beardall. "What would be the best deal you could make me on this place? Remember, I'm going to have to use some of my own money for repairs."

Mr. Beardall nods. "I know." He thinks about it for a minute. "The best price I could let you have it for would be $44,000. I'd sell it to you for that price if you would give me $10,000 in cash as a down payment. It already has a mortgage of $34,000. I'm only asking $10,000 cash for my equity."

"That seems fair enough," says Mike. "Give me a couple of weeks and let me see what I can do about getting the $10,000 cash together for you."

Mike looks the house over carefully and decides he will need about $3,000 to fix the place up for resale. When repairs are completed he thinks he can resell it for about $50,000.

He decides that he will go to a mortgage broker in this case. He will only need about $3,000 to fix the house up, but thinks that he had better borrow $4,000 just to be on the safe side. To run short of money before he has the house fixed up would be disastrous.

He decides to go to a mortgage broker instead of a bank because the mortgage broker does not look at the purchase contract. He only wants to know how much equity you have in the house.

First, he goes back to Mr. Beardall and talks with him again. "First," he tells him, "I'm going to have to borrow this $10,000 from a mortgage broker to get you the money for your down payment. I'm also going to borrow $4,000 for repairs. Let's do this. You want $44,000 for the house. That's fine. I'll assume the mortgage at $35,000 and give you your $10,000 cash. But, I need a $4,000 refurbishing fee added to the official selling price of the house, and that will make the official purchasing price of the property $48,000. I'll borrow $14,000 from the mortgage broker, you'll get the $44,000, and I'll have $4,000 left over to use for refurbishing."

Mr. Beardall goes along with the deal. As long as he gets his $44,000, $10,000 of it in cash for his down payment, everything is fine with him.

Mike buys the house on these terms. He actually has to spend only $2,800 to renovate the house. He has $1,200 cash left from the $14,000 he borrowed from the mortgage broker. He puts the house up for resale and in three weeks a buyer pays him $51,000. He has made a profit of $3,000 between his own purchase price of $48,000 and his resale price of $51,000. Add to that the $1,200 left of the money he borrowed for the refurbishing fee, he has an actual total profit of $4,200.

Discounted Bonds

78

Randy Jones has found another apartment complex for sale. This one has 14 units. After he has made all his calculations concerning rental income, his mortgage to Mr. Gibbons and to the bank, Randy negotiates the best deal he can. He knows this will be a profitable deal for him in the long run.

The trouble is, Mr. Gibbons wants a whopping down payment. Even after Randy has calculated in the rental security deposit, the escrow fund for real estate taxes, and the one month of rental payments from the tenants, he still needs $20,000 more in cash to meet Mr. Gibbons' demands for a cash down payment.

Again, he could go to Mr. VanFleet and he is sure Mr. VanFleet would put up the money for this venture. But, Randy would really like 100% of this apartment building, if he can get it. He has been reading books on real estate investments and he has attended a couple of good seminars. Somewhere in all this reading and listening he has learned something about discounting bonds.

He says to Mr. Gibbons, "All right, you want $20,000 more as a down payment. Will you accept $20,000 in negotiable bonds?"

"Bonds? Well, yes, bonds are very solid as an investment. Yes, I'll take bonds for the rest of that down payment."

"All right," says Randy. "Let's get all this down in writing, just to make it legal." They write into the purchase contract that the remaining $20,000 of the down payment shall be acceptable by Mr. Gibbons in the form of $20,000 worth of bonds.

Randy knows he can get big discounts in buying bonds for cash. He checks and finds that he can indeed buy $20,000 worth of bonds (face value maturity) for $10,000 right now. They will not mature for years to come, but when they do mature, they will be worth $20,000.

He goes down to a bank and talks to the commercial loan officer. He takes out a $10,000 commercial short term loan. He uses this $10,000 to buy $20,000 worth of bonds. Now he takes the bonds and gives them to Mr. Gibbons for the rest of the $20,000 down payment. This way he is able to buy the property.

Once the property is legally in his name, he goes back to the bank and puts a $10,000 mortgage on it. He uses this $10,000 mortgage to pay off the $10,000 commercial short term loan which saves him $20,000 worth of cash down payment on this apartment building. He has made a very large down payment without using any cash of his own.

79   Option To Buy Discounted Notes

Randy Jones is out looking for single family houses again. He likes the apartment buildings for rental income, but he likes the single family houses for buying and reselling quickly. He has learned to hunt not only for good buys in houses, but also for good buys in discounted mortgage notes.

Today he finds a house that looks interesting. It does not look too good, and the yard is covered with weeds. The whole place looks shabby and definitely shows a lack of interest by the owner.

He goes in to talk with the owner, Mr. Krebbs. The property would be worth about $50,000 if fixed up right. Randy thinks he could do this by spending $1,000 or less. He asks Mr. Krebbs, "What is the lowest price you would take for your house?"

"$47,000," says Mr. Krebbs. "And, I won't take a penny less."

"Do you have an assumable mortgage?"

"I guess so," the owner replies.

"Who holds the mortgage?" asks Randy.

"The Arlington Bank. You can go ask them about it."

Randy does just that. He goes straight to the Arlington Bank and starts talking with the loan officer, Mr. Bartholomew. Mr. Bartholomew says, "Yes, the loan is assumable, but you'll have to qualify for it. We've got to make sure you are able to make these monthly payments."

He frowns at the mortgage note in front of him. "We've had trouble in the past."

Randy looks at him carefully. "Have you had some problems with Mr. Krebbs making his payments in the past?"

"I'd rather not make any comment on that," says Mr. Bartholomew.

But that tells Randy what he needs to know. The bank does not consider Mr. Krebbs a very good risk. "Mr. Bartholomew, would the bank be able to sell me this mortgage note at a discount? I'd pay cash for it."

Mr. Bartholomew brightens up considerably at this offer. "Why, yes, I think that could be arranged."

"Would you give me a 50% discount on it?"

"No, not that much. But we would sell it to you for 60% of the face value. The value of the mortgage is a little over $39,000 right now."

"All right," says Randy. "Let's make out the papers now. We'll make it a one year option to buy."

The bank gives Randy an option to buy the $39,000 mortgage note at 60%, which comes to $23,400. Before he has even bought the house, Randy has already made a profit of $15,600!

80   If Seller Sells To Someone Else

Now that Randy Jones has obtained the option to buy the mortgage on Mr. Krebb's house, he goes back to talk to him again. He does not say anything about getting the option to buy Mr. Krebb's mortgage note, but when they are making out the purchase agreement, Randy writes in a clause to the effect that any prepayment of this mortgage note on the house will be to the benefit of the buyer and not the seller.

Mr. Krebbs says, "I don't want to sign this purchase agreement yet. I want to talk to my lawyer about it first. Come back and talk to me again in a few days." Randy goes home and hears nothing from Mr. Krebbs for several days. He decides to go over in person to pay Mr. Krebbs a call.

When he arrives, he goes up to the door and knocks. The door opens and Mr. Krebbs stands there, glaring at him. "So! You thought you could buy out my mortgage at a discount, did you? I've got my lawyer working on this case right now! I'm going to buy my own mortgage back at a discount myself! And, I'm going to cut you out of this deal without a red cent!"

Randy does not know quite what to say to this. Mr. Krebbs continues, "Now you just hit the bricks! I've got a new buyer in here and I'm showing him the house." Randy walks away from the house thinking, "Well, you can't win 'em all . . . "

He goes home and tries to forget the whole thing. Three days later he receives a call from Mr. Bartholomew, the loan officer at the Arlington Bank. He wants Randy to come down and see him at his earliest convenience.

Randy goes down to the bank and Mr. Bartholomew says, "I have good news and bad news for you. Which would you like first, the good news or the bad news?"

"Give me the bad news first," says Randy. "Let's get it over with."

"The bad news is that Mr. Krebbs sold his house to another buyer, so you lost out on owning his house."

"Now, are you ready for the good news?"

"What good news?" asks Randy.

"Here's the good news on my desk." He picks up a piece of paper and hands it to Randy.

Randy stares at it. It's a cashier's check made out to Randy Jones in the amount of $15,600!

"What happened?" he asks. Mr. Bartholomew says, "When Mr. Krebbs tried to cut you out of everything and sold his house to another buyer, this mortgage was paid off. It had to be paid off. So you end up with cash for the $15,600 we discounted you on that mortgage."

Randy loses out completely on buying Mr. Krebbs' house and finds himself "stuck" with $15,600!

Discounted Mortgage Note As Down Payment 81

This discounted mortgage business really impresses Randy Jones. He tells Mr. Bartholomew, "I'm really interested in buying more of these mortgages at a discount. Does your bank have other mortgages that you might be willing to sell for cash at discount prices?"

Mr. Bartholomew says, "We may have some more in the future. I'll bring this up at the next meeting and if we have anything that might interest you, I'll give you a call."

Randy goes to several other banks and makes the same standing offer. He is willing to buy their mortgages for cash at discount rates. He also puts an ad in the newspaper: WILL PAY CASH FOR YOUR MORTGAGE. He runs this ad in the real estate section.

Eight days after he has placed the ad in the newspaper, he receives a phone call. "Hello, are you the one who wants to buy mortgages?"

"Yes. My name is Randy Jones and I'll pay cash for your mortgage if I can buy it at a discount."

"What percentage are you willing to pay in cash?" The caller asks.

Randy is not quite sure. "That all depends on the mortgage and the property. I'll have to see both." Randy wants to buy mortgages at discount prices, but he does not want to get stuck with a lemon. He knows that the house the mortgage is covering should be worth the money owed on the mortgage, and that the person paying off the mortgage a month at a time should be willing and able to make the payments every month. He meets with the holder of the mortgage, looks it over, and goes out to look at the property. The house seems to be in good condition. The people who are living in the house seem to be nice. They also appear to be able to make their monthly payments with no problem.

Randy goes back to the holder of the mortgage. "All right, Mr. Washburn, I'm willing to pay you cash for your mortgage note. I'll pay you 65%."

Mr. Washburn counters, "That's not quite enough. I'd like at least 70%."

Randy knows that the house is good, the mortgage is good, and the people are good. "Okay, in this case I'll go ahead and pay you 70%. Let's sit down and make out a purchase agreement on this mortgage note."

They do, and Randy writes into the purchase agreement that he will purchase this mortgage note subject to financing. This means he has an escape clause if he cannot come up with the financing necessary to buy this mortgage. Randy now controls this mortgage. He knows that no one else can buy it out from under him. This gives him the security he needs to go ahead with the rest of the deal as planned.

The mortgage note he is buying is a $20,000 note. He is buying it at 70%, so he is paying $14,000 in cash for it. With this figure in mind, he goes out and finds a two family unit for sale at $80,000. It has a $40,000 mortgage on it, and the owner, Mr. Green, has $40,000 worth of equity. Randy says, "If I buy your place, Mr. Green, will you let me pay monthly payments on your equity?"

"Some of it," says Mr. Green. "If you'll pay me $10,000 cash down, I'll give you a second mortgage for $30,000."

"That's fine with me," says Randy, "if you'll let me give you a $20,000 mortgage note on another property for $20,000 worth of your equity in this house. I'll give you $10,000 down in cash, and my own $20,000 mortgage on this other house. That will leave $10,000 equity in your place, for which I'll give you back a $10,000 mortgage note."

"That sounds just fine," says Mr. Green. They sit down and make out the purchase agreement to this effect.

Randy now goes down to the bank and gets a new loan on the property he is buying, a loan for 80% of the value of the house. 80% of $80,000 is $64,000. So he takes the loan for $64,000. He uses $40,000 of this money to pay off the old mortgage on the place he is buying. He then goes back to Mr. Washburn and pays him $14,000 in cash for his $20,000 mortgage. Then he goes to the seller, who is selling him the $80,000 two-family unit, and gives him this $20,000 mortgage note he has just purchased, plus $10,000 down in cash. This is part of the $64,000 cash which he borrowed from the bank. Then he signs the mortgage note for $10,000 over to Mr. Green to cover the rest of the equity in the house he is buying.

Randy Jones has bought an $80,000 two-family house, and has an instant equity of $6,000. $6,000 is the amount he was able to discount off the $20,000 mortgage when he bought it at a price of $14,000.

He now has an $80,000 two-family house with $6,000 worth of equity in it and he has done this without paying a dime of his own cash!

82   Creating Your Own Discounted Mortgage

Randy Jones is getting good at discounting mortgages. He has learned them forwards and backwards. He has a new idea on how to create his own discounted mortgage if none is available.

He finds a $70,000 home with a $45,000 mortgage on it. The seller, Mr. Audubon, is willing to deal with Randy.

Randy asks, "Are you willing to take monthly payments on your equity?"

The owner doesn't know. "I've got a lot of equity built up in this place. $25,000 worth of equity. I was hoping to get most of it in cash. I'll tell you what I'll do though. If you give me $15,000 down in cash, I'll take a $10,000 mortgage note on the rest of the equity."

Randy accepts the deal. He goes home and looks through the newspaper, searching the classified ads in the real estate section. He finds an ad which reads: MORTGAGES BOUGHT FOR CASH. This is similar to his own ad. But, he needs another mortgage discounter right now. He can work this deal.

He calls the number in the ad. A man answers. "Hello. I saw your ad in the newspaper today. Are you the one who buys the mortgages?"

"I'm the one. I'm Henry Ridge. Do you have a mortgage you'd like to sell for cash?"

"Yes, I do," replies Randy. "It's a new second mortgage. Do you buy that kind?"

"Yes, but I'd have to take a look at it before giving you a final decision."

"That's okay," says Randy. "I'd like to come over and talk to you in person about it."

They make an appointment for later in the afternoon at Mr. Ridge's office. Randy wants to talk to him in person rather than over the phone. He walks into Mr. Ridge's office. "Mr. Ridge, I'm Randy Jones. I came over to talk to you about that second mortgage I mentioned over the phone."

"Yes, let's have a look at it."

"I can't show it to you yet," says Randy. "It isn't written up. But it will be a new second mortgage and I want to sell to you at $15,000 cash."

"What! Now wait just a minute here. Before I buy a mortgage from you, you've got to give me its face value and the interest on it. Also, I need to know when it's due to be paid off in full."

"Not in this case. I want you to tell me what the face value of the mortgage should be, and the interest payable on it, and when the mortgage should be finally paid off, in order for you to give me $15,000 cash for the mortgage note." Mr. Ridge laughs.

"Oh, I see what you're up to now. You want to work it backwards, do you? All right, give me a minute and I'll figure it."

He works on his desk calculator, tapping in the numbers. "All right, in order for me to give you $15,000 cash for a new second mortgage, I would need to have a mortgage with a face value of $19,000 at 12% interest, with a payoff date of six years."

"Then that's exactly what you'll get," says Randy.

Randy goes back to Mr. Audubon and explains the situation to him, they sit down together and write out a mortgage note for $19,000 on Mr. Audubon's property. A note with 12% interest and a payoff date six years from now.

"Now," says Randy, "we'll take this $19,000 mortgage note to Mr. Ridge, and he'll give you $15,000 cash for it. You have $25,000 equity in your property here, so this mortgage note will pay off $15,000 of that in cash. Finally, I'll give you a $10,000 third mortgage note on the rest of your equity."

"Okay," says Mr. Audubon. "This note will actually give me $15,000 in cash." He then looks at the $19,000 mortgage note with 12% interest, with the payoff date of six years from today.

"Hmmm," he says, "this mortgage note would give me $4,000 more on my property plus 12% interest."

He looks up at Randy. "On second thought, I think I'll just keep this $19,000 mortgage myself. Is that all right with you?"

"That's just fine with me, it doesn't make a bit of difference whether I'm paying these monthly payments to you or to Mr. Ridge."

You will be *amazed* to see how many sellers will change their minds on the second mortgage for $19,000!

Borrowing On The Certificate Of Deposit

83

Linda Richardson has no cash, no credit, and no property. She wants to go into real estate investment. She has been out looking for good deals in houses. She has found several, but all the owners want some money down in cash, cash she does not have.

She decides she had better see if she can borrow down payment money from a bank. She goes in and talks with a loan officer. After checking out her income as a secretary at the university, and seeing that she has nothing to put up as collateral, the loan officer shrugs and says, "I'm sorry, Miss Richardson, but the bank cannot give you a commercial loan, or any other kind of loan at this time."

Linda asks, "What would be the interest rate if I could get a loan?"

"That would be $15\frac{1}{2}\%$ for a commercial loan and $14\frac{1}{2}\%$ for an installment loan secured against your collateral. But as I said, you just don't have enough collateral to apply for a loan at this time."

Linda sighs, "Thank you, anyway." As she is walking through the bank on her way out, she overhears a conversation between one of the bank officers and an irate customer. "I'm sorry, Mrs. Whitaker, but if you withdraw all your money from this certificate of deposit now, you'll lose the interest on it."

Mrs. Whitaker says, "When I signed up for this certificate of deposit two years ago, that 9% interest looked really good. Now you're paying 10% on the same certificates. I've got $20,000 in this certificate and I want to change it to take advantage of the new 10% rate."

The bank officer tries to look patient. "As I said before, Mrs. Whitaker, you're tied into that 9% interest. That was the agreement when you signed up to take out the CD. We can't raise the interest on it now. You've got to wait until it matures in two years. Then you can take out a new CD at whatever prevailing interest will be then."

"Then you mean there's no way I can get my $20,000 out of this certificate of deposit without losing all my interest?"

"Well, if you need some money from the deposit, we can lend you back what money you need, we'll charge you 1% interest above the interest we're paying you on the certificate of deposit." Mrs. Whitaker turns red in the face. "Thanks, but no thanks!" She turns and heads for the door.

Linda falls in beside her and starts chatting. "I couldn't help hearing that, Mrs. Whitaker. I have an idea that I think you'll like. I think I can show you how to get a higher interest rate on your certificate of deposit."

"Oh?" says Mrs. Whitaker. "Just what do you have in mind?"

"I'm a real estate investor," says Linda. "I need some ready cash for down payment money. I heard you say you wanted to get 10% interest on your certificate of deposit. I'd be willing to give you that 10% interest, if you will borrow $10,000 out of your CD. That's 1% above the 9% the bank is giving you. Then, I'll borrow that $10,000 from you and pay you 11% interest on it. That will leave you with a net interest of 1%. Add that to the 9% the bank is already paying you on your CD and you'll have your 10% interest."

"Yes, I see how it would work," says Mrs. Whitaker. "But what would I have for security?"

"I can give you good security," says Linda. "In the first place, I'll give you a lot more than just the 10% interest on your money. I'll give you a 25% interest in the property I am buying with it. Whenever I resell it, you'll get 25% of the profits. And, if it will make you feel any better, I'll even give you a quit claim deed for my 75% of the property as security for the money I've borrowed from you. Right now, I want to borrow the $10,000 as a down payment on a nice six-unit apartment complex. How would you feel having a six-unit apartment building as security for your $10,000?"

Mrs. Whitaker smiles, "I'd feel very secure about it." They go ahead with this arrangement, and Linda is able to buy the apartment building. Best of all, she now knows a ready source of cash at a much lower interest rate than the banks will charge, and without having the usual forms of collateral banks demand. She is purchasing a fine six-unit apartment building with no money down of her own. Best of all, now she has a method she can use over and over again to raise money for her real estate investment.

Moving Private Mortgage From Senior Position To Junior Position

84

Randy Jones has found another good buy. This time it is a two-family house owned by Mr. Peterson. They negotiate and settle on a purchase price of $80,000. Mr. Peterson says, "I'm giving you a good price for this property. If I give you this price, I want all cash for my equity. Can you pay me all cash?"

"If I can swing it," says Randy. "You already have a mortgage on the place, don't you?"

"Yes, it's owned by a man named Harris. It's valued at $40,000."

Randy is glad to hear this. He likes privately owned mortgages. They are always good possibilities for buying at a discount. He goes to see Mr. Harris. "I'd like to buy your mortgage from you, Mr. Harris. I'll pay you 60% cash for that mortgage."

Mr. Harris shakes his head. "No deal." He seems very set about this.

Randy tries a little different approach. "I'll give you $20,000 cash, and pay off half your mortgage note if you are willing to move that mortgage from a first to a second mortgage. You will have $20,000 cash and you will still have $20,000 left on your mortgage note, but now it will be a second mortgage note."

Mr. Harris thinks it over. "Okay, if you give me $20,000 cash, it's a deal."

Randy gets this in writing signed by Mr. Harris. He has learned always to get everything in writing and signed by both himself and the other person. He now goes back to Mr. Peterson, the owner. Together they draw up and sign a purchase contract.

Randy now begins his next step. He goes to the bank to refinance the building with a new first mortgage. The two-unit building is worth $80,000, and the bank is willing to lend him 80% of this value, or $64,000. He borrows only $60,000, because he knows this is all he will need. He uses $40,000 from the loan to entirely buy out the equity of Mr. Peterson. This leaves him $20,000, which he uses to buy out half of Mr. Harris' mortgage on the house. Then he gives Mr. Harris a $20,000 second mortgage on the property.

Randy has now bought this two unit-house, worth $80,000, and has a $60,000 first mortgage on it with the bank and a $20,000 second mortgage on it from Mr. Harris.

He has done this while spending not one penny of his own money!

85   Making Mortgage Holder Your Partner

This time Randy Jones has found a real buy! A nice four-plex near the university and the owner will sell it to him at a price of $80,000. The apartments are not big, but they are all right. They will rent, especially to students and younger couples. All of the units are rented at the present time and Randy knows he won't have any trouble keeping these units filled, even out of season.

Randy asks all the usual questions. The owner has a $50,000 first mortgage on the complex and $50,000 in equity. He knows he is giving Randy a bargain price on the property. Therefore, he wants all cash for his $50,000 equity. "To find out if the mortgages are assumable, you'll have to go talk to Mr. Jarvis. He's the one who holds the mortgage on the place."

Great news for Randy! Another private mortgage holder! He loves to deal with private mortgage holders.

He locates Mr. Jarvis and talks with him. "Mr. Jarvis, I'll pay you cash for your mortgage if you'll give me a discount on it."

Mr. Jarvis shakes his head. "Sorry. I'm not interested in selling it. I like the monthly income it provides."

Randy tries again with a new technique. "If you won't sell it, then how about letting me pay you cash for half of it. I'll pay you $25,000 cash and leave you with a $25,000 mortgage. Then I would like you to move that from a first mortgage to a second mortgage."

Mr. Jarvis responds, "Sorry, I'm not really interested in that offer, either."

Randy Jones is a very persistent person. He is always trying to think of a different way of doing things when other ways don't work. "How about this. I'm going to buy this four-plex from Mr. Clark. He's agreed to my terms, and we both signed the purchase agreement. How would you like to get in on this deal with me, as a partner? I'll give you 50% interest in this property. You'll get 50% of the tax benefits on the depreciation and 50% of the appreciation in the equity buildup. All you will have to do is temporarily cancel this $50,000 debt to you and when I refinance the property with a new first mortgage from the bank,

I'll give you a new second mortgage at 75% of the value of your old first mortgage. Seventy-five percent of $50,000 is $37,500."

"Why do you want me to temporarily cancel my first mortgage?"

"Because," explains Randy, "if that mortgage is on the property, I'll never be able to refinance it at the bank. But I'll sign a legal paper for you that will put your new mortgage into effect as soon as the refinancing loan comes through. In other words, all I'm asking you to do is to move your first mortgage to a second mortgage and reduce it from $50,000 to $37,500. That's just a drop of $12,500. For that $12,500 drop in your mortgage value, you get a 50% interest in the property itself. You get the advantages of being a property owner instead of a mortgage holder. You also get 50% of the appreciation."

"There are just two more things I want to know," says Mr. Jarvis. "As owner of a 50% interest in this property, am I liable for 50% of the mortgage payment to the bank, and, am I responsible for 50% of the mortgage payments to myself?"

"No," Randy reassures him. "I'll be liable for all mortgage payments, both to the bank and to you. I will do all the managing of the property and the handling of the rentals. I will, however, get all the money from the rentals, because I'll need that money to make the mortgage payments."

Mr. Jarvis nods. "That sounds like a good, fair deal." Mr. Jarvis temporarily removes his mortgage from the property altogether, and Randy goes down to the bank and gets a new $50,000 first mortgage on the property. He uses all this $50,000 cash to pay Mr. Clark for his equity. Then he gives Mr. Jarvis a $37,500 second mortgage.

Randy Jones and the seller now own this $100,000 four-unit apartment building jointly. It has a $50,000 first mortgage to the bank, a $37,500 mortgage to Mr. Jarvis, and an equity of $12,500 in the property. Randy Jones has now bought a four unit apartment building worth $100,000. He already has an equity of $6,250 in it, and he has accomplished this without paying a dime of his own cash!

Getting Them Something They Want (Besides Cash)   **86**

Mike Dugan is a friendly guy. He genuinely likes to chat with people, particularly sellers of property. He is talking now to Mr. Gavin, owner of a medium sized rental house in a respectable neighborhood on the west side. "Yes, it is a nice house, Mr. Gavin, why are you selling it?"

If Mike had asked him this in the beginning, he might have been offended. But now that Mike has chatted with him for half an hour, he is more talkative and friendly. He answers, "Oh, I'm just tired of managing a rental house. Besides that, we could use a little extra cash to fix up some things around our own place." Mike files this answer away carefully in his memory. It could be useful later.

He asks, "What is the lowest price you could afford to give me on your house? I want you to be happy with the deal, and if I can afford to buy it, I will."

Mr. Gavin pauses then says, "$47,000. Could you afford to buy it at that price?"

"Maybe. The price is right. If the terms are right, too, then I can buy it."

"What kind of terms are you talking about?"

"First, I have to know if you have an assumable mortgage, and second, if you're willing to take monthly payments on your equity."

"Oh. I have a $28,000 mortgage with the bank. At a selling price of $47,000, that leaves me with an equity of $19,000, and yes, I would be willing to take monthly payments on my equity. But I do want $3,500 cash as a down payment."

Mike had been preparing for this. He is naturally friendly and has a good rapport with the seller. He knows from their conversation that Mr. Gavin wants to do some fixing up around his own home. He thinks probably this $3,500 down payment has something to do with it. He says, "$3,500 is quite a chunk of cash for me right now. Do you have to have that much right away?"

"Well, my wife wants a new kitchen put in. She wants the old cabinets torn out and replaced, and a new stove and refrigerator. She wants the whole thing redone from the top to the bottom."

"And that will cost $3,500?"

"Yes, I called a contractor and that was the price that he quoted me."

"Is there any plumbing involved?"

"Oh, no. Nothing like that. Just general carpenter work and painting up afterward. She wants new tile laid in the counter too.

Mike says, "In other words, Mr. Gavin, what you want the down payment money for is that new kitchen for your wife?"

"Yes."

"All right, then. I'll get that new kitchen put in for you. If I do that, will you give me credit for a $3,500 down payment?"

Mr. Gavin looks surprised. "Why . . . I don't know . . . I suppose if the kitchen came out okay, it would be all right. My wife would have to approve it, of course."

"Good enough. I'll get that kitchen put in and she'll love it." Mike pulls out a purchase agreement and starts writing it up. "Let's get all this in writing. In exchange for a kitchen your wife will approve, you'll give me credit for a $3,500 down payment on this house."

They write it up. Mike goes to work on Mrs. Gavin's kitchen. He tears out all the old cabinets and puts in new ones. He has worked construction before and knows basically how all this is done. Whenever he needs some technical advice, he talks to one of his contractor friends. He lays the tile and paints the entire kitchen, and even installs a new stove and refrigerator. The new stove and refrigerator cost him $760 altogether. He buys them on monthly installments from the appliance store.

Mrs. Gavin is completely happy with her new kitchen and Mike receives credit for $3,500 as a down payment on the seller's rental house. Mike Dugan has bought a nice rental property with no cash down.

Using A Lien On The Property To Get Them What They Want

87

Mike Dugan has found another good buy. This one is a duplex rental. The owner has advertised it at $70,000. Mike is sure it is worth at least $73,000. He does not try to talk the owner down, because he believes he has already come down to $70,000. There are two families living in it now, one in each side, and they seem happy living there.

He says to the owner, "Mr. Bryce, I'd like to buy your duplex. I figure your price is just about right, and I'm willing to pay it. However, the only way I can buy it is if you will take monthly payments on your equity. If you're willing to do that, we can make a deal right here and now."

"I have $32,000 worth of equity in this duplex. How big would your monthly payments be on that?"

"I can pay 1% per month," says Mike. "That would give you payments of $320 a month. I'll also pay 10% interest. That will give you about three times your $32,000 in the long run."

"That's true," agrees Mr. Bryce. "But I've still got to have some cash up front. I need to have at least $6,000 cash down."

Mike continues to talk with him for a while in his friendly, courteous manner. Then he says, "I couldn't afford $6,000 cash right away. Do you really need all that money now? Is there something special you need it for?"

"Well, yes we do. My wife and I want to buy a motorhome. We found a good deal on one for $6,000 and want to buy it."

Mike thinks this over. "If I can get you that motorhome at no cost, will you let me have $6,000 as a down payment credit on buying your house?"

"Why, sure. That's what we wanted the $6,000 for in the first place. Get us that motorhome and I'll forget that down payment."

They sit down together and make out the purchase agreement. They write into it that this motorhome will be used as the down payment on the property. Then Mike goes out to negotiate with the owner of the motorhome. The man who owns it is a private owner, not a dealer. Mike asks, "What is the least amount you would take for your motorhome, Mr. Larsen?"

"Well, I was asking $6,000 for it. But I'd be willing to settle for $5,000, if you'd give it all to me in cash."

"I can't do that," says Mike. "I'll have to give you monthly payments on it. I'll give you interest of 10% on it and give you monthly payments of $100 a month until it's paid off, principle and interest together."

Mr. Larsen looks hesitant. "I already lowered the price to $5,000 for you, and that was if you'd pay cash."

"You're right," says Mike. "I'll pay you the whole $6,000 for your motorhome, plus 10% interest on top of that—in monthly payments of course."

"That sounds a lot better," says Mr. Larsen. "But what kind of security will I have for my money? I don't want this motorhome as security, because it's got wheels. It could be 1,000 miles away from here in a couple of days."

"You're right again," says Mike. "I'll tell you what I'll do. I'm purchasing a nice property, a duplex rental for $70,000. I'd be willing to give you a lien on that property to secure your $6,000 loan to me on your motorhome. We can put that all in writing, if you like. Your lawyer can write it up."

"I'd like that. Having my lawyer draw up papers for a lien on your $70,000 duplex gives me a lot of security for my $6,000 loan."

Again, the seller has bought a very nice piece of property using no cash of his own. The seller of the property is happy, because he and his wife are getting what they wanted in the first place, a nice motorhome.

Sweat Equity 88

Mike Dugan is out looking for good deals again. He finds an ad in the newspaper on a deal that looks like a good buy. It is a four-plex being offered for $70,000. He calls the owner and arranges to drive by the place and see it.

When he locates the place, he knows why it's being sold for $70,000. This four-plex is a wreck! The roof is sagging and patches of shingles have been torn off in places. The paint is peeling and some of the windows are broken. The front yard has gone to weeds and there are piles of junk lying everywhere. What was once a giant picket fence around the property is now lying in ruins.

Even so, Mike decides to investigate. He walks up to the house and reaches for the doorbell. He notices the button is missing and a bare wire is lurking just inside the cavity, waiting to strike. His better judgement tells him to knock.

A worried looking man opens the door. "Hello, I'm Mike Dugan. I called about your house."

"Oh, yes. I'm Mr. Garnie." He shows Mike through the house. All of the apartments need to be repainted and recarpeted.

Mike is hesitant about this whole deal. However, there is one thing that makes him think this might end up a good buy. Fixed up, this property should be worth $100,000. This could be a means of a real profit for Mike. "I'm very interested in your place, Mr. Garnie. It does need some work, but I'd be willing to pay you the $70,000 you're asking for it. I'd have to assume your mortgage and give you monthly payments on your equity. If you agree to those terms, I can proceed to buy your place right away."

Mr. Garnie says, "I have a mortgage of $42,000, and I know you can assume it. I checked with the bank. I'm selling it to you for $70,000, so that gives me $28,000 in equity. I'd be willing to give you a second mortgage for $18,000 on the building if you can give me $10,000 in cash."

Mike shakes his head. "$10,000? I couldn't handle that much cash. Besides that, I think that's too much to ask as a cash down payment for this place."

"Well," says Mr. Garnie. "I'm asking $10,000 in cash because I know if you pay that much down, you're not going to walk away from it later. When I sell this place, I want it sold."

"I understand." Mike replies.

"I think we can deal with each other. I'm willing to give you a $10,000 down payment if you're willing to let me give it to you in sweat equity."

"Sweat equity? What's that?"

"Sweat equity is the work you put into a house to fix it up. Of course, that includes the cost of the materials you've got to use in fixing the place up. I'm willing to give you $10,000 of fix up time, labor, and materials as a $10,000 down payment credit in buying your property. It will take about a year to do everything that needs to be done, so I'll want to be able to do it over the course of a year. We can write it into the purchase contract and I'll do my best to get it done as quickly as I can."

Mr. Garnie thinks hard about Mike's offer. Then says, "Now wait a minute. I'm not getting anything out of this deal. No down payment money at all. You're deducting that $10,000 worth of sweat equity, as you call it, from my selling price! This is a good deal for you, but it doesn't do me any good at all!"

Mike says, "It will do you a lot of good, Mr. Garnie. In the first place, you can't sell this building at a price of $70,000. Nobody will buy it. It's the type of place that when people see it, they take one look and just keep driving. That's just about what I did. I think you will be a long time in trying to sell this place at that price unless you fix it up. You've got to either fix it up yourself or lower the price, or else let me come in with my $10,000 worth of sweat equity. How long have you had this place up for sale at this price?"

Mr. Garnie looks uncomfortable. "It's been awhile," he admits.

"I thought so. This place can stay on the market forever at this price unless it's fixed up; nobody's going to buy it when it's in this condition, especially at that price."

Mr. Garnie nods. "I think you're right."

Mike continues, "I've got only so much money. If I pay $10,000 cash to you, I'll have no cash left to make the needed repairs. The place will still be in bad condition and I won't be able to rent it out or sell it." Mike goes on, "But, if you let me come in here with my $10,000 of sweat equity and fix it up right, this four-plex is going to be worth $100,000. I'll not only have my $10,000 in sweat equity in this place, including some of my materials which I will have to buy with my own money, but I'll have $30,000 more in equity. This will give you real security. I'm certainly not going to walk away from a deal where I have $40,000 worth of equity."

Mr. Garnie agrees. "I can see what you're saying is true."

"Sure, it's true," says Mike. "And another thing, I'll be giving you a second mortgage of $18,000 on the place. If you ever want to use it as collateral to get a loan from a banker or other lender, he's going to drive by here and take a look at this four-plex. If it looks the way it does now what do you think your chances will be of getting a loan? But, if I fix it up the way I intend to, any banker will gladly give you a loan based on your mortgage note."

"I get your point," says Mr. Garnie.

"One more thing," adds Mike. "After I put $10,000 worth of time and money into this place, I've got a much stronger chance of refinancing the property or reselling it to get my money back out of it. Either way, you're going to be paid off in full in your mortgage note."

That does the job. Mr. Garnie is convinced. Mike and Mr. Garnie sit down and fill out the purchase agreement and Mike gets credit for $10,000 on his sweat equity. Sweat equity can be a powerful tool in buying property, especially fix-up property.

Pay Full Price If Seller Accepts Well Secured Note For Equity

89

Randy Jones has sold one of his homes and has a $20,000 mortgage note remaining on that particular property. The new buyer is paying him monthly payments on it. He continues to go out and look for new real estate to buy. He finds a nice five-plex and talks to the owner, Mr. Walden. Mr. Walden says he will sell the building for $100,000 even. Randy looks the place over and concludes it is a good, fair price. He asks, "Do you have an assumable mortgage?"

"Yes, I have a mortgage on it for $80,000, and you can assume it. My equity in it is $20,000, and I'd like that $20,000 in cash, all at once."

Randy says, "If you really want all cash for your equity, I'll give it to you, but at a total selling price of $92,000. This will give you $12,000 in cash for your equity." Randy knows he can take this mortgage note to a mortgage buyer and get at least 60% on it. That would give him $12,000 cash. He could then use this cash to buy out the equity in Mr. Walden's five-plex.

Mr. Walden shakes his head. "$12,000 isn't enough," he insists. "I have $20,000 worth of equity and I would like $20,000 for it."

"In that case," says Randy, "I can give you the $20,000, but not in cash. I'll give you the $20,000 in the form of a well secured mortgage on a single family dwelling. It's a good solid mortgage note. If you'll accept this for your equity, I'll give you your full asking price of $100,000 for your property."

Mr. Walden thinks it over. He likes the move back from $92,000 to $100,000. He agrees.

Always remember, equity can be negotiated up and down. Mortgage notes can be discounted from their face value down. When you are trading mortgage notes for equity try to trade straight across so you are getting a dollar's worth of equity in exchange for a dollar's worth of the face value on your mortgage note.

90

The Numbers Game

As we have learned, Randy Jones is a very persistent person. Everyday he looks in the newspapers and checks out the real estate ads. He circles the ads that interest him and calls the owners. If a phone call tells him the house and the owner seem promising, he makes an appointment to see the property.

Today he is checking out another one. Everything is average about this house; it is not in great condition, but it is not in poor condition. It is an ordinary house in the middle of the middle income group. He talks with the owner, Mr. Beal. "What is the lowest price you could give me on your house, Mr. Beal?"

Mr. Beal says, "The price I listed in the ad was $55,000. I'm not going to take anything less than that."

"Do you have an assumable mortgage?"

"No, I'm afraid I don't. I talked to the bank, and the loan officer said that when I sell this house the mortgage has to be paid off immediately. It's called a 'due-on-sale clause.' You'll have to refinance the whole thing yourself."

"I'm sorry, too," says Randy. "I guess I won't be able to buy your house."

Randy leaves, and goes on to the next place he wants to see. Like the first, this home is an ordinary looking place in the middle income group. He talks with the owner, Mr. Brown, and makes sure that the house has an assumable mortgage. At $52,000, the price is right too. He asks, "Mr. Brown, are you willing to take monthly payments on your equity?"

Mr. Brown shakes his head. "No, I've got to have cash for my $18,000 equity. I wouldn't take monthly payments under any circumstances."

"All right," says Randy, "I can't buy your house, but thank you for showing it to me."

Randy leaves and drives on to the next house on his check list. It looks much like the other two he has just looked at, just a medium sized house in a middle class neighborhood. He talks to the owner, Mr. Hammond, and asks him the usual questions. The price of the house is $54,000, and it has an assumable mortgage of $32,000. This gives Mr. Hammond an equity of $22,000.

Randy asks, "Mr. Hammond, are you willing to take monthly payments on your equity? I'll give you 10% interest and make payments of 1% per month. That would be $220 a month. In the end, you'll get three times as much money for your equity as if I paid you the entire $22,000 at once."

"That sounds all right to me. I'll take your monthly payments on my equity." Mr. Hammond does not even ask for a down payment. They write up the purchase contract and Randy buys the house with no money down.

Randy goes home that night and looks through his records. He has been buying a lot of houses lately. He has run into a lot of dead ends, where the house was just not right, the price was not right, the loan was not assumable, or the owner would not take monthly payments on his equity.

He decides to see what his "batting average" is. He goes through his records and discovers that for every 15 houses he looks at, he will make offers on six. Out of these six offers, one will be accepted by the seller.

This is encouraging. He decides there is no way of controlling which of the 15 houses he looks at will be good enough for him to make his six offers, and, there is no way of knowing which one of his six offers will be accepted. But he does see clearly that for every 15 houses he goes out to look at he will buy one.

This is what you can do as a real estate investor. You are going to develop a certain "batting average." It may not be exactly the same as this, but it will be some kind of average. Once you find out what this average is, you can control the number of houses you buy by the number of houses you look at and make offers on.

91   Buy And Sell At Same Price, And Make Money!

Randy Jones has just made a good buy on a single family dwelling at $50,000. He is paying the owner 10% interest on the mortgage the seller has carried back on the property. He is making monthly payments of $480.

Randy decides to try another experiment. He puts the house up for resale, advertising in the newspapers, putting up signs on bulletin boards, and putting a FOR SALE sign in the front yard.

A young couple came to look at the house, and liked it. Randy does not feel that he can raise the price on this house to make a profit. It is just a $50,000 house. When the man asks how much he wants for the house, he replies, "$50,000."

"What kind of terms could you give us?" asks Mr. Brewster.

"I'll give you excellent terms." replies Randy. "I'll take monthly payments at 11$1/2$% interest, giving you co-payments of $550 a month."

Mr. Brewster says. "Yes, we can afford payments like that." Then he looks a little worried. "I hope you don't need a big down payment."

"I don't," says Randy. "I got a good deal on this place and I'll pass it along to you. I won't ask you for any down payment."

The Brewsters are delighted! "We'll take the place on those terms," says Mr. Brewster.

They write up the purchase contract.

Randy is buying this house at 10% interest, making monthly payments of $480 a month. He is selling it to the Brewsters at 11$\frac{1}{2}$% interest, and receiving payments of $550 a month. This gives him a net income of $70 a month.

He is selling the house at the same price that he bought it for. But because he is paying 10% interest, and is charging 11$\frac{1}{2}$% interest, he is getting a monthly profit of $70. Once he has discovered how to do this the first time, Randy does it over and over again, building up a steady monthly income from buying and reselling houses at the same price, but receiving a higher interest rate.

Houses, 20% Off! 92

Randy Jones has become a firm believer in the law of averages. He is also a believer in percentages. He knows that a certain percent of all sellers are "Don't Wanters." They don't want their property and they will sell it at a real discount just to get rid of it.

He decides to try another experiment. He knows that a house can be refinanced at 80% of the fair market value. This means that if he can buy a house at 80% of the fair market value, he can refinance the house later with a loan equal to the price he actually paid for the property. This is equivalent to buying the house with no money down. He does not know how many "Don't-Wanters" there are out there, but he knows there are some.

Randy really goes after mass volume now. He checks out all the ads in the newspapers, calling every one and making appointments to see the houses.

Every time he goes out to look at a house, he makes the same offer—20% below the fair market value. He does not negotiate or argue with the seller. He simply says, "Mr. Cox, I'll give you $40,000 for your house. I'll pay all cash."

Mr. Cox says, "Are you kidding? This house is worth $50,000. I'm not about to sell it for $40,000."

"All right," says Randy. "Thank you for showing me your house."

Randy leaves and goes to the next place on his list. He goes through many "no" answers.

He comes to a house with a fair market value of $50,000 and makes the same offer he has been making to all the others. "Mr. Crenshaw, I'll give you $40,000 for your house. I'll make you 1% per month payments on your equity." Mr. Crenshaw looks surprised at first, but then considers the offer. On the surface, Mr. Crenshaw does not seem any different from any of the other sellers. His house is not in bad condition, but Mr. Crenshaw is a "Don't Wanter." He does not want this property. He wants to sell out and get out.

He says, "All right, Mr. Jones. I'll take your $40,000."

Randy writes up the purchase agreement and leaves, going on to the next house on his list. He works quickly, moving from one house to the next, making his offers of 20% below the fair market value. He does not stop to argue or negotiate with anyone. He keeps moving from house to house, making his offers quickly. By the end of the month, he has bought eight houses, all at 20% below the fair market value. This gives him room to work. Two of the houses need to be refinanced; he has no trouble doing this, because he has bought them at 20% below the fair market value. When the houses are appraised, the banks give him loans of 80% of the appraised value on these properties. This gives Randy 100% of the purchase prices on these houses.

Twenty percent off the fair market value is such a good deal that Randy can resell these houses quickly and still make a profit. Even when he has to refinance, he is still buying these houses with no money down.

Buying And Selling On Contract 93

The tables are turned and Randy Jones has a house for sale. He has bought it with no money down, and is offering it for resale, no money down. He is listing this one with a real estate broker at a price of $60,000.

One day the phone rings. "Hello, Randy?"

"Yes."

"This is Dave at Bernhard's Realty. I've just sold your house."

"Great! I'll be right over." Randy meets with him.

"They're giving you your full asking price," says Dave.

"All right! How soon do I get the money?"

"As soon as the buyers can qualify for their FHA loan."

"How long will that be?" asks Randy.

"These people are well qualified, and the FHA should approve them in two weeks or so."

Four weeks and three days later, the phone rings again. "Hello, Randy. This is Dave again. Great news! The FHA has approved the buyers for your house."

"Just as soon as the FHA approves your house, they'll be sending out an inspector any day now." Two weeks later the inspector finally arrives. He goes over the house thoroughly and takes notes.

A week after that, the inspection report arrives. It has a detailed list of all the things that need to be fixed about the house before it will pass inspection. The list is five pages long, single spaced!

One month, two more house payments, and $2,000 in fix-up costs later, Randy has his house ready for his second go-round with the FHA inspector.

Two weeks later the re-inspection report comes in. It says in order for the house to pass its final inspection he has to remove a little dirt touching one of the basement window sills. In total frustrations, Randy hops into his car and drives all the way across town. As he kicks the dirt away from the window sill, and makes believe it is the FHA inspector.

Another house payment comes due. His buyers, the Andersons, are getting really anxious to move into his house. Randy is very anxious to get his money. He thinks they are ready to complete the deal right now.

Surprise! There is still another player in this game—the banker!

Randy calls the bank every day or two. One of the escrow officers keeps telling him everything is ready to close, but, for some reason the bank seems to be stalling.

Another month and another house payment later, the phone rings. The escrow officer says, "You can come down to the bank and sign your papers now and get your money." Within 60 seconds flat, Randy is in the car heading for the bank. When he gets there, he finds out the bank is giving him over $2,000 less than his original agreement. He asks about this, and the escrow officer calmly tells him that during the time it took to close the deal the seller's points have risen from one and one half points to six points! This has added another $2,250 to Randy's closing costs!

When buyers use FHA or VA loans to buy houses, the banks charge sellers percentage points called "points." The banks charge these extra points to make up for the lower interest rates they are giving the buyers. This is great for buyers, but tough on sellers, especially tough when the bank deliberately delays the closing until they are legally able to raise the points!

He looks the loan officer right in the eye and says, "Mr. Shrever, just who do you think you're kidding? I know you've been deliberately delaying this closing until you could raise the points on me!" Mr. Shrever looks back at him and smiles.

"I'm not going through with this deal at all!"

Mr. Shrever smiles again, "Then we'll sue you for nonperformance."

"I'll be back tomorrow," says Randy. "I'm going to go have a talk with my lawyer about this," He knows this whole affair may drag out much longer, and the bank will probably beat him in court, forcing him to go through with the deal. Meanwhile, he will still be making these monthly property payments. Suddenly he realizes just how much power these banks have. He sees the Andersons coming into the bank. They smile at him, and he tries to smile back. When Mr. Shrever gives them their papers, the Andersons are just as shocked as Randy. "Why, you've raised the interest rate on us!" exclaims Mr. Anderson. "This is a higher rate than we have in that contract."

Mr. Shrever explains calmly, "I'm sorry, but your closing date has gone beyond the interest rate commitment period. The bank has had some extra costs lately. The bank has raised its interest rates on all loans."

Then Mr. Shrever smiles at the Andersons. "But we can't pay these higher monthly payments," says Mr. Anderson. The steel plant laid off another bunch of workers and I was one of them. I've got another job, but it doesn't pay as much as the steel plant."

Coldhearted Mr. Shrever stops smiling. His face turns red. "What?! Then we'll have to have you fill out a financial statement all over again to see if you qualify for the loan."

It doesn't take a month to qualify them this time. After less than five minutes of questions and answers, the beady-eyed banker says, "That's it. There's just no way you can qualify for this loan, not even FHA."

The Andersons look relieved. Randy laughs and says, "What Mr. Shrever means is that you just lost your qualifications to get skinned alive by the bank." The Andersons laugh and leave the bank with Randy, leaving Mr. Shrever sitting red-faced behind his desk.

As they walk into the main part of the bank, Randy says to the Andersons, "Look, if you still would like to buy my house, let's just deal with each other and forget all about the banks and the FHA."

Mr. Anderson says, "Yes, I think I'd much rather deal with you than with this bank."

"All right," says Randy. "I've had to spend $2,000 more on the house to meet those FHA requirements. If you will give me the $2,000 as a down payment, I'll let you pay off my equity in monthly payments. I'll also charge you less interest than this bank. Just give me a second mortgage on the place as security for my equity."

Mr. Anderson says, "You're a lot easier to deal with than either the FHA or this bank. But for now, let's get out of here before the bank starts charging us rent for standing on their floor space!"

Building A Real Estate Money Machine!

94

After his great adventure with the frowning FHA inspector and the smiling Mr. Shrever, Randy resolves to get back in control of his own deals. He definitely needs to avoid costly entanglements with banks. His solution is this: from now on he will buy and sell only with a private contract—100% of the time!

Soon after this incident, another buyer comes along and wants to buy from him through FHA. He has $14,000 in the property. If he waits for the buyer and his house to get FHA approval, and maybe has to spend a few thousand dollars to meet their requirements, he may have to wait five or six months before he ever receives his money.

He sits down at his desk with his pocket calculator and does some figuring. Suppose he just sells this house on his own contract, receiving monthly payments on his own equity. He can get his down payment back through the new buyer and invest this initial payment again and again. If he buys and resells the house quick enough, his calculations show that in five months, the time he would probably have to wait to get his money through the FHA loan, he could build up total equities of $150,000 in properties! These $150,000 in equities would net him $1,200 a month in payments. He decides to see what he can do with this idea in the next five months.

He goes to the buyer who wants to buy this house FHA and says, "Mr. Vernon, I have a better deal for you than you could get from the FHA or the bank. If you give me a $4,000 down payment on my house and a second mortgage on my equity you can pay off my equity in monthly installments, at 10% interest."

Mr. Vernon agrees. Randy takes this $4,000 down payment from Mr. Vernon and applies it as a down payment on the next house he buys. He fixes the house up and has it back on the market inside of a week.

The house sells for a $10,000 profit! Randy receives $6,000 down. He now has an equity of $6,000 in the house and is receiving a net income of $50 a month on this equity. It has taken five weeks from the day he offered to buy the house until the day he sold it, five weeks to buy and resell, instead of five months of pain and aggravation in dealing with the FHA and the bank.

Randy would much rather deal with someone his own size. The banks and the government are much too big for him. The people who are his size are just other people. If he can continue to work with other people instead of institutions he stands a much better chance of controlling his progress.

Randy uses the $6,000 he has received as a down payment on the sale of his last house to make down payments on the purchases of two more homes. He is dealing with people here, not institutions, and he closes each one of these transactions within two weeks of his purchase offers.

Randy continues to buy and sell houses, getting his down payment money back every time he resells a house to a new buyer. He always buys on contract with the seller, giving monthly payments for the equity, and resells on contract with the new buyer. He sells the house at a higher price, which gives him added equity in each house. Selling each home at a higher price allows him to build his equity in each house he buys. He is also receiving a net income each month from each one of these equities.

This is quick work. Sometimes he resells a house within a few days after he has bought it. Once he received an offer from a new buyer before he signed the final purchase papers with the seller he is buying the house from. He accepted the offers, receiving the usual $6,000 profit in his equity.

At the end of five months, Randy Jones has over $150,000 in equities, which are netting him over $1,200 a month! His experiment is a success.

Randy has learned his lessons in real estate very well. He is buying into the middle of the middle income class, where by far the greatest number of buyers are. He is also buying at a low enough price so he can still pass on this good deal to the next buyer. Therefore, he can quickly resell each house he buys. He is doing something that can be duplicated over and over again.

Randy Jones has created his own real estate money machine!

Cash Value Life Insurance: A Rich Source Of Money   95

Sometimes you will need a "grub-stake" to help you get going in real estate investment. Maybe you have found a wonderful deal. You know you can resell it quickly, get your down payment back, and get those steady monthly payments coming in to you through that money machine. There is just one catch. You don't have the small down payment required to buy that first house. What do you do? You tap into one of the most abundant supplies of dormant money in this country—cash value life insurance policies.

This is how it works. Life insurance companies charge people far too much on their premiums leaving them a great deal of money just stashed away.

So how can you tap into this rich supply of money? You simply borrow it back from the life insurance company. You have to pay interest on this money, but it is a very low interest rate compared to the interest rate you could get anywhere else. Usually these rates will be only 3 to 6% maximum. You can borrow this money on your own cash value life insurance policy, if you have one. Otherwise, you can get someone else to borrow on their policy.

Here is an example: approach someone who wants you to be a success, someone who has a stake in you. This could be your father, mother, uncle, or an aunt. The person could be just a good friend.

Let's say your Uncle Charlie has a $30,000 life insurance policy which he bought years ago that now has a cash value of $12,000. He can borrow this money from the life insurance company at 5% interest. You tell your Uncle Charlie that if he borrows that money for you, you'll pay him 10% interest. This is twice as much interest as he is paying on it.

You might even be able to negotiate a lower interest rate than this, if your Uncle Charlie really likes you.

Suppose you borrow $10,000 from him. If he were to die the very next day, how much money would the insurance company pay his beneficiary or beneficiaries? The insurance company would pay $20,000 on this policy. They will be very careful to take their $10,000 loan back from the total of $30,000.

If this should happen, your Uncle Charlie's estate would lose $10,000. Of course, you would not want this to happen. This is what you can do. You buy him a $10,000 term life insurance policy. If he is 50 or 60 years old, it might cost $300 a year. If he is 34 years old, it would cost about $50 a year.

Tell your Uncle Charlie that you will take $1,000 of the money he is lending you to buy a three year term life insurance policy for him.

Now, should anything unforeseen happen to him, his beneficiaries will get $20,000 from the life insurance company and the additional $10,000 from the term policy, a total of $30,000.

However, you might have a problem here. Your Uncle Charlie might be built like a Sherman tank. He might jog three miles a day and have the blood pressure of a teenager. He may have lived a lot of years, and intends to live a lot longer.

He takes a good look at you. He wonders just how much longer you are going to last! He may start thinking of all the horrible ways you could die, and that you just might not live long enough to repay his loan.

What can you do to allay his fears? You can always promise him faithfully to stay away from junk food, tobacco, alcohol and drugs. You can promise him you'll start jogging three miles a day, and assure him that you will be careful while driving your car. You can also go out and buy a $20,000 term life insurance policy on yourself. Then, if you die before you can repay the loan $10,000 of your policy will go to pay him back, and the other $10,000 can go to your wife.

Suppose you borrow this $10,000 for three years. You then buy term life insurance policies of $20,000 on both yourself and your Uncle Charlie, both for three years. Suppose Uncle Charlie is paying 5% interest on his loan from the insurance company. At the end of three years he will have paid the life insurance company $1,500 in interest. But, you have been paying him twice as much interest—10%. He will have received $3,000 from you in interest during those same three years.

Uncle Charlie has made a clear profit of $1,500. Think of what you could do with that $10,000 during those three years! If you bought houses with an average of $2,000 down payment plus closing costs and fix up, you could have bought a total of five homes. If you bought these properties and sat on them for that period, they would appreciate in value a great deal, particularly if you did a good job in the first place and bought them right.

If you purchase and resell them with the money-machine concept, you will get those steady monthly payments coming in to you every month, building up your monthly income. You will also be getting your down payments as you resell the houses.

You can use your original down payments to buy other properties, and continue to build your monthly payments.

With this in mind, you could make your Uncle Charlie an even better deal. You could offer him a percentage of whatever your total profits are during those three years. You could give him 10, 20, or maybe even 25% of your actual profits. What you are doing is borrowing someone else's money, and no matter what happens, you are going to make that person wealthier than he was before.

There are literally billions upon billions of dollars just sitting out there dormant in all those cash value life insurance policies. Most people who own those cash value policies don't even know that extra money out there really belongs to them. Even if they do, they may not know how to get it until they die, then, only their beneficiaries will get it.

Your job is to go out and find people with these cash value life insurance policies, explain that the money is there, and that it is available to them. Then borrow this money at a fair interest rate.

What do you do if you don't know anyone who owns a cash value life insurance policy? You ask your friends and relatives first, of course, and then systematically ask other people.

However, there is a great source for finding these cash value life insurance policies that is unfortunately often overlooked.

This source is the life insurance agent! Any life insurance agent probably knows great numbers of people who own these cash life insurance policies. Now, why should he give you the names and addresses of all these people? Simple. He is going to make a lot of money on your deals.

You propose this: if he lines you up to borrow money from his clients who have these cash value life insurance policies, you will pay interest on this money. Tell him about the two brand new term life insurance policies he is going to be able to sell every time you borrow money out of one of his client's cash value policies. The life insurance agent will work with you on your deals. Money is a great motivator!!

The Option To Buy

96

Randy Jones has found another nice buy in a one family house. It's in a nice residential section and he can resell this one quickly if he can get a fair price on it. He asks the owner, "What is the lowest price you could give me on your house and still be happy with it?"

Mr. Beckman thinks for a moment. "I think $55,000 would be about right."

With just a little touching up in places, Randy is sure he could resell this house for $60,000. He asks the usual questions and finds out there is an assumable mortgage of $31,000, leaving Mr. Beckman with an equity of $24,000.

Randy offers, "Will you take monthly payments on your equity? I'll give you a second mortgage on the place as security."

Mr. Beckman says, "I've got to have at least $4,000 cash as down payment. If you give me that much up front, I'll let you have the rest of the equity in monthly payments."

"All right," says Randy. "Let's put this down in writing." He does not have the $4,000 in cash himself, but he knows Mr. VanFleet would go along as his partner on this deal.

Then he has another thought. "I don't have the $4,000 in cash right now, but I can get it for you fairly soon. What I'd like to do is get an option to buy your place for $55,000, and according to the terms we agreed upon."

"An option to buy? How long would you want that option?"

"I'd like to get it in writing for a year," says Randy.

"I'd be willing to give you an option to buy, but at this price, only for six months."

"All right," says Randy, "that seems fair enough." They write up an option to buy that is good for six months. Randy has this house tied up, so no other buyer can purchase it out from under him. He thanks Mr. Beckman.

With an option to buy, Randy has taken this house off the market and put it under his control. He has done this without making the $4,000 down payment and without making any monthly payments.

He has six months to come up with the down payment. He knows he can always go to Mr. VanFleet or Esther and Irv, but, he wants to buy this house on his own if he can.

Once Mr. Beckman has moved out, Randy puts the house up for resale. He shows the house to six potential buyers. The last one really wants it. He asks, "How much do you want for your house, Mr. Jones?"

Randy replies, "$60,000. There's an assumable mortgage on it for $31,000. I have $29,000 equity in it."

"Do you have to have all that equity paid off in cash?"

"Well, I would like a $6,000 down payment. I'd be willing to let you pay off the rest of it in monthly installments at 10% interest."

"Fair enough. I'll buy it." Randy fills out a purchase agreement with him and receives $6,000 cash as a down payment.

He goes to Mr. Beckman and pays him the $4,000 down payment Mr. Beckman had asked for, and exercises his option to buy the house.

With this option to buy, Randy has resold the house before he has even officially bought it. He has picked up the down payment money plus $2,000 extra from his new buyer. This is not only a no money down deal, it is a money in your pocket deal!

Section 9

Ways
To Find
Good Deals

Ways To Find Good Deals

I am not the first one to think of this idea, nor am I the first one to put it into action successfully, but I do it consistently. Always remember, only do that which can be duplicated.

I am talking about a model, a system. Every morning, you get up and get started. From 8:00AM to 9:00AM you look through the newspaper circling ads that look like good deals. From 9:00AM to 11:00AM you go out and look at 22 houses. From 11:00AM to 12:00 you meet with the real estate agent to plan your afternoon. Go have lunch, and in the afternoon, hit it again. Go look at another 13 houses. Every day, you make at least four offers on the houses you've seen.

If you follow this system every day, what do you think will happen by the end of the week?

You're going to find houses. You're going to create systems that can be duplicated. If you do this, you will be a success!

Continually analyze your work, refine it, define what you are doing, and you will continue to get better at it.

Always remember this: you don't need 1,001 ways of buying real estate. You only need a few good ways that work for you! Start using these consistently, and you will be off and running!

As you have already seen, there are quite a few ways you can work directly with a seller rather than banks and other institutions. You have an idea of what interest rates are good and how much you are willing to pay. Now I have another angle to show you. When you toss out an interest rate of 10%, what will the seller usually counter offer? If you said 11 or 12%, you're right. What if you were to offer an interest rate of 9.25%? Would that put the seller into a different mindset, thinking of increases in fractions rather than whole numbers? You bet! This is another one of my favorite negotiating techniques. If you usually start at 9%, begin starting at 8.25% or 8.75%. If you can negotiate with incremental increases, it can save you money in the long run.

You are on your way to success!

Interest Rates And Monthly Payments You Can Live With

97

Suppose you get a great no money down deal on a good piece of property. Does that solve all your problems?

Not by a long shot. There are two things that you have to watch closely: interest rates and monthly payments.

Let's look at interest rates first. Never pay 12% interest. You are not dealing with a regular bank or a savings and loan. You are dealing with a private seller. You do not have to pay the interest rates to a private seller that you would have to pay to a bank.

If you tell the seller you are going to make a banker out of him and he wants to charge you the same interest rates that the bank would charge, point out to him, "Don't look at the interest rate the bank is charging its customers, look at the interest rate the bank is giving its customers. I will give you more interest on this loan than the bank would ever pay you on your savings account." Let him think that over. Then, gently but firmly explain. "It's against our principles to pay 12% interest." Then negotiate a lower interest rate. Try to get a rate of 9% to 11.5%, or even 11.75%. But never pay 12% interest.

Let me tell you about a four-plex I bought recently. Each unit has five bedrooms and 1600 square feet. This four-plex was two years old and appraised at $165,000.

I offered $130,000. The seller agreed, but wanted $10,000 down. That was too high a down payment for me. I offered to pay $5,000 down now and $5,000 at the end of two years. This would equal the $10,000 down payment the seller wanted. She agreed.

However, she insisted on receiving 12% interest on her loan to me, with payments of $1,400 a month.

I insisted on 11% interest on the loan and $1,200 monthly payments.

We haggled back and forth. I told her, "I will never pay 12% to buy any property."

Finally, we agreed on an interest rate of 11.75%. Why never 12% interest? Because 12% or more interest will not amortize at a monthly payment rate of 1% of the balance.

98   Interest Up Monthly Payments You Can Live With

A seller has just agreed to let you buy his house with no down payment and you have negotiated a good interest rate below 12%.

Is this all you need in order to be safe? Again, not by a long shot. You have got to set up monthly payments that you can live with. More real estate deals have gone sour because of high monthly payments than any other factor.

Let's look at an example. Suppose someone had $10,000 equity in a house. What is the most you would be willing to pay per month? One percent per month is your absolute limit. This would make monthly payments of $100. But what happens if this is going to cause you a negative cash flow? You could offer the seller some alternatives.

You could offer to pay nothing for the first year and then pay $100 a month. Or, you could pay $50 per month for the first year, $100 per month the second year, and $150 per month thereafter.

Another alternative is to offer to pay $20 per month the first year, $40 per month the second year, $80 per month the third year, and then $100 per month thereafter. Over four years you would build up to $100 a month.

These are called graduated payments and they let you buy a property without suffering negative cash flow in the beginning.

Whenever you are setting up monthly payments that you know you can live with, always remember that when you offer the house for resale you want to give a good deal to the person who buys it from you. You will want your new buyer to pay you more money per month than you are paying on your loan, but the person who buys the house from you is going to have to live with his monthly payments too.

Whenever you are thinking about buying a property, don't think just "first generation;" think "second generation." Consider how this house will be for the renter or buyer who lives in it. Always get low monthly payments so that you will be able to pass low monthly payments on to your buyer, even after you have added your monthly profit to his payment. Find houses that fit your model so that you will be able to buy and sell with low monthly payments.

Always remember this: monthly payments determine your staying power in real estate investing!

An Exciting Idea 99

I want to tell you about a property I bought that helped me develop the exciting new concept below.

I found a property for sale at a price of $30,000. The seller wanted only $1,000 down. The problem was the shabby, unkept look that made the house unattractive to a buyer. I talked to my fix-up crew, who estimated it would cost from $2,000 to $2,500 to clean up.

I asked, "If we fix it up right, how much is it going to be worth?"

They said, "Probably $41,000 or $42,000." Does this sound good to you? You would be buying the house for $30,000 and spending about $2,000 to fix it up. If you sold the house at $42,000 you would be making $10,000 clear profit.

Then, if you work the money machine, you will be getting $100 a month profit on the new buyer's payments to you. One percent of $10,000 is $100. This is what your net profit will be on your payments coming in over and above your payments going out.

This would be profitable, but let's look at another alternative. How much could you sell this house for right now without bothering with repairs? Your reason for selling immediately would be to get your $1,000 down payment back, plus some quick profit. Could you sell it for $34,000 with $1,000 down right now?

If you sell this house for $34,000 at $1,000 down, the new buyer will owe you $33,000 after he has paid you the $1,000 down. You will still owe $20,000 on the house. This will give you a $4,000 note from the new buyer, which will give you $40 a month, at 1% per month.

This way, you have no money buried in this property. You also have your $1,000 down payment back.

With this program, you can spend your time buying and selling houses profitably rather than working with crews and repairing the fixer-uppers. Just go for it and get it done.

Consider another alternative. If you can sell a house for $30,000 with $1,000 down, could you sell it at a price of $36,000 or $37,000 with nothing down? Let's say you sell it for $37,000 with no money down. The new buyer owes you $37,000, and you still owe $29,000 to the former owner. The difference between $37,000 and $29,000 leaves you with a $8,000 profit. This can give you an $8,000 note, and at 1% a month, you will be getting monthly payments of $80. However, you will have the $1,000 cash down payment buried in this deal. This $1,000 cash that you have invested in the property is buying you an extra $4,000 worth of mortgage note from the new buyer. In the first alternative, you sold the house at $4,000 less, but with $1,000 down. You recovered your initial investment of $1,000. In this alternative, you sold the house at a price $4,000 higher, but did not ask for a down payment.

Consider a third alternative. If you fixed up this house right, you could sell it at its real market value of $42,000. You can deduct $1,000 from the market value, reducing the selling price by $1,000. Offer the new buyer $1,000 to use in fixing up the place. Sign an agreement to reimburse him as he fixes up the house, up to a total of $1,000.

You will now have $2,000 cash in this property, $1,000 down and $1,000 fix-up. You still owe $29,000 on the property, and the new buyer owes you $41,000. The difference here is $12,000, giving you a $12,000 note. At 1% a month, you will be getting payments of $120 a month coming in to you. That extra $1,000 invested in the property is buying another $4,000 worth of mortgage notes, along with an extra $40 a month income.

Let's take a good look at these three alternatives. Which one of these alternatives is really best for you? If you get your $1,000 payment back, you have no cash buried in the property and you will have a $4,000 mortgage note yielding $40 per month to you. If you leave your $1,000 down payment in the property, you end up with an $8,000 mortgage note yielding you $80 a month. If you leave your $1,000 down payment in the property and add another $1,000 fix-up cost, you have $2,000 invested and a $12,000 mortgage note, yielding you $120 a month. No cash buried gives you a $4,000 note. $1,000 invested gives another $4,000 mortgage note and another $40 a month.

You would be better off to take that extra $1,000 and go get another $8,000 note.

Now consider this. You could take that $8,000 note and sell it. You can discount some of your equity, and sell that note for cash. There are people who advertise in the newspapers that they buy discounted mortgages, deeds of trust, and contracts.

How much could you get for this $8,000 note if you discounted it? Probably $4,000. You can usually receive 50% of the face value of your note if you sell it at a discount. If you hang onto the note for a couple of years, you could probably get $5,000 or $6,000.

Say you buy the house on Monday, and you got a good deal. You sell it Wednesday and pass the good deal along to a new buyer. You have an $8,000 mortgage note on the sale of the house. Friday you sell your note at a discount. The people who buy the note will drive past the property and do a title check. This will take a day or two. The title insurance for buying a note like this costs from $29 to $35. It takes one or two days to process the whole thing. On Tuesday or Wednesday of the following week, they will give you a check for $4,000. This is 50% of your $8,000 note. You deed the note over to them. They are now collecting the payments from the buyer of the house and making the payments you would have been making. You are completely out of the picture as far as this house is concerned, and you have $4,000 in your pocket. How much did you start out with on this particular deal? One thousand dollars. You used $1,000 to make your original down payment on the house. This means you have made a clear profit of $3,000 in one week.

The Power Of Being In Control   **100**

You now have $4,000. You could take $1,000 of this and do the investment all over again. You could use $1,000 and buy one rental property and hang on to it.

You could simply keep your $8,000 mortgage note and live on the monthly payments from it. You could take that $8,000 mortgage note and use it as a down payment to buy another property. You might even use that $8,000 note as a down payment on a $100,000 four-plex.

The point is this: you are in control of your own situation. What put you in control? You went out and made a good enough deal on buying the house that you were able to make another good deal to the buyer who bought the house from you. Since you are in control of the situation, you can dictate the terms of how you receive that profit and what you will do with it. You have a wide range of alternatives, and every one of them is to your advantage.

Another point: you may find a piece of property that is not such a good deal in the beginning, but you can make that property a good deal by using one of these 101 ways.

Don't wait for inflation to build up the value of your property. You can build in your own property value increases. Every time you go out to look at a property, say to yourself, "How can I maximize this? How can I get the most out of this property?"

Nothing Happens Until You Make An Offer   **101**

You may be able to set up a deal allowing you to make no monthly payments at all for a while. The secret is in negotiation.

Before you enter into any negotiation, decide where you really want your final offer to be. Then start somewhere below that. If the seller does not want to accept your first offer, you can negotiate with him and raise your terms a little, ending up where you wanted to be in the first place.

Let's take an example from my book **Real Estate For Real People**. I had a client who called me all the way from Philadelphia. He had just found a tremendous deal on a four-plex. He wanted very much to buy it. The selling price was only $40,000, and the real value of the property was $80,000. This was only 50¢ on the dollar. The existing financing included an assumable loan of $20,000, leaving an equity of $20,000 for the seller.

I asked my client, "How does the seller want his $20,000 equity?"

"Of course," my client replied, "he wants it all in cash."

I asked, "What would you like to pay?"

He answered, "I'd like to pay him his $20,000 in two years." I said, "Okay, that might not be too bad. But why does he want to do that? Why do you want to pay him a lump sum of $20,000 two years from now?"

"Because that's one of the techniques I learned at a seminar."

I said, "Do you really want to do that? Do you really want to be responsible for coming up with $20,000 two years from now?"

"No."

"Then how about offering him this deal? Ask him if he is willing to take $200 a month for his $20,000 until it's paid off?"

"Yes," said my client. "I really like that idea."

Then I asked, "Do you really want to pay him $200 a month right now?"

"No."

"Well, why don't you ask him if you can start paying him $200 a month two years from now?"

"No," he admitted.

"Then why don't you make him this offer? You don't pay him anything at all for two years. Then give him $100 a month through the third year. Raise it to $150 a month through the fourth year, and then raise your payments to $200 a month for the balance of the loan."

"That sounds like a great idea. That's the way I really would like to buy the property." This is what he wrote into the earnest money agreement.

Now, what is going to happen when he walks into the room and makes this offer to the seller? The offer is going to hit him right between the eyes.

Still, even if the seller does not accept this offer, several things are accomplished here. One is that he started low enough that he will be able to negotiate with the seller and gradually come up to something that would be more comfortable for both of them. The most important point is that he is starting *below* where he wants to be. This allows him room to raise his offer during the course of negotiation.

No matter what happens now, this initial offer is going to start the negotiating process. The purpose of negotiation is to get right down to business and start discussing what the seller can afford to take and what the buyer can afford to give. This gives both the seller and the buyer a good understanding of exactly what the other can afford.

Now that they understand each other, they are prepared to make an application of what they have learned, and they can sit down and put together an agreement.

One final note: do not be afraid to ask questions or to make an offer that you think might be embarrassing. You just might be surprised. An offer that you might feel is way out of line might be totally acceptable to the seller.

Always figure out exactly where you would really like to be, and then make the offer *you* want to make.

Section 10

Available Resources

Available Resources

The following books, videos, and audiocassettes have been reviewed by the Wade Cook Seminars, Inc. or Lighthouse Publishing Group, Inc. staff and are suggested as reading and resource materials for continuing education in financial planning and real estate and stock market investments. Because new ideas and techniques come along and laws change, we're always updating our catalog.

To order a copy of our current catalog, please write or call:

Wade Cook Seminars, Inc.
14675 Interurban Avenue South
Seattle, Washington 98168-4664
1-800-872-7411

Or, visit us on our web sites at:
www.wadecook.com
www.lighthousebooks.com

Also, we would love to hear your comments on our products and services, as well as your testimonials on how these products have benefited you. We look forward to hearing from you!

Audiocassettes

Income Formulas-A free cassette
By Wade B. Cook

Learn the 11 cash flow formulas taught in the Wall Street Workshop and how to double some of your money in 2½ to 4 months.

Power Of Nevada Corporations-A free cassette
By Wade B. Cook

This powerful seminar teaches individuals how to use Nevada Corporations for privacy, minimal taxes, no reciprocity with the IRS, and asset protection.

Income Streams-A free cassette
By Wade B. Cook

Learn to buy and sell real estate the Wade Cook way. This informative cassette will teach you how to build and operate your own real estate money machine.

Money Machine I & II
By Wade B. Cook

Learn the benefits of buying and more importantly, selling real estate. Money Machine I & II teach the step by step cash flow formulas that made Wade Cook, and thousands like him, millions.

Money Mysteries of the Millionaires-A free cassette
By Wade B. Cook

This fantastic seminar shows you how to use Nevada Corporations, Living Trusts, Pension Plans, Charitable Remainder Trusts, and Family Limited Partnerships to protect your assets.

Unlimited Wealth Audio Set
By Wade B. Cook

Unlimited Wealth is the "University of money-making ideas" course that shows you how to make more money, pay fewer taxes, and keep more for your retirement and family.

Retirement Prosperity
By Wade B. Cook

    This audiotape set walks you through a system of using a self directed IRA to create phenomenal profits, virtually tax free.

The Financial Fortress Home Study Course
By Wade B. Cook

    This series helps structure your business and affairs so that you can avoid the majority of taxes, retire rich, escape lawsuits, bequeath your assets to your heirs without government interference, and, in short, bomb proof your entire estate.

Paper Tigers and Paper Chase
By Wade B. Cook

    In this set of six cassettes, Wade shares his inside secrets to establishing a cash flow business with real estate investments. Learn the art of structuring your business to attract investors and bring in the income you desire through the use of family corporations, pension plans, and other legal entities.

Books

Wall Street Money Machine
By Wade B. Cook

    Appearing on the *New York Times* Business Best Sellers list for over one year, **Wall Street Money Machine** contains the best strategies for wealth enhancement and cash flow creation you'll find anywhere.

Stock Market Miracles
By Wade B. Cook

    The anxiously awaited partner to **Wall Street Money Machine**, this book is proven to be just as invaluable. This is a must read for anyone interested in making serious money in the stock market.

Bear Market Baloney
By Wade B. Cook

   A more timely book wouldn't be possible. Don't miss this insightful look into what makes bull and bear markets and how to make exponential returns in any market.

Real Estate Money Machine
By Wade B. Cook

   Wade's first best selling book reveals the secrets of Wade Cook's own real estate system—the system he earned his first million from. This book teaches you how to make money regardless of the state of the economy.

How To Pick Up Foreclosures
By Wade B. Cook

   This book will show you how to buy real estate at 60¢ on the dollar or less. You'll learn to find the house before the auction and purchase it with no bank financing. This is the easy way to millions in real estate.

Owner Financing
By Wade B. Cook

   This is a short but invaluable booklet you can give to sellers who hesitate to sell you their property using the owner financing method. Let this pamphlet convince both you and them.

Real Estate For Real People
By Wade B. Cook

   A priceless, comprehensive overview of real estate investing, this book teaches you how to buy the right property for the right price, at the right time. Wade Cook explains all of the strategies you'll need and gives you 20 reasons why you should start investing in real estate today.

Brilliant Deductions
By Wade B. Cook

   Do you want to have solid tax havens and ways to reduce the taxes you pay? If so, this book is for you! Learn to structure yourself and your family for tax savings and liability protection.

Blueprints for Success, Volume 1
Contributors: Wade Cook, Debbie Losse, Joel Black, Dan Wagner, Tim Semingson, Rich Simmons, Greg Witt, JJ Childers, Keven Hart, Dave Wagner and Steve Wirrick
Blueprints for Success, Volume 1 is a thorough look at what success is and how to achieve success in the stock market.

Wealth 101
By Wade B. Cook
This incredible book brings you 101 strategies for wealth creation and protection that you can't afford to miss. Front to back, it is packed full of tips and tricks to supercharge your financial health.

Videos

Dynamic Dollars Video
By Wade B. Cook
Dynamic Dollars is Wade Cook's 90 minute introduction to the basics of his Wall Street formulas and strategies. Wade explains the meter drop philosophy, Rolling Stock, basics of Proxy Investing, and writing Covered Calls.

Build Perpetual Income (BPI)-A videocassette
Wade Cook Seminars, Inc. is proud to present Build Perpetual Income, the latest in our ever expanding series of seminar home study courses. In this video, you will learn powerful real estate cash-flow generating techniques such as power negotiating strategies, buying and selling mortgages, writing contracts, finding and buying discount properties, and avoiding debt.

Wall Street Workshop Video Series
By Wade B. Cook

If you can't make it to the Wall Street Workshop soon, get a head start with these videos. These ten albums contain 11 hours of intense instruction on Rolling Stock, Options on Stock Splits, Writing Covered Calls, and eight other tested and proven strategies.

The Next Step Video Series
By Team Wall Street

This is the advanced version of the Wall Street Workshop. Full of power-packed strategies from Wade Cook, this is not a duplicate of the Wall Street Workshop but a very important partner. You'll learn how to find the stocks to fit the formulas through technical analysis, fundamentals, home trading tools, and more.

Classes Offered

Cook University

People enroll in Cook University because they are a discontented with where they are—their job is not working, their business is not producing the kind of income they want, or they definitely see that they need more income to prepare for a better retirement. The backbone of the one-year program is the Money Machine concept—as applied to your business, to stock investments, or to real estate. Although there are many, many other forms of investing in real estate, there are really only three that work: the Money Machine method, buying second mortgages, and lease options. Of these three, the Money Machine stands head and shoulders above the rest.

If you want to be wealthy, this is the place to be.

The Wall Street Workshop
Presented by Wade B. Cook and Team Wall Street

The Wall Street Workshop teaches you how to make incredible money in all markets. It teaches you the tried-and-true strategies that have made hundreds of people wealthy.

The Next Step Workshop
Presented by Wade B. Cook and Team Wall Street

An Advanced Wall Street Workshop designed to help those ready to take their trading to the next level and treat it as a business. This seminar is open only to graduates of the Wall Street Workshop.

Executive Retreat
Presented by Wade B. Cook and Team Wall Street

Created especially for the individuals already owning or planning to establish Nevada Corporations, the Executive Retreat is a unique opportunity geared toward streamlining operations and maximizing efficiency and impact.

Real Estate Workshop
Presented by Wade B. Cook and Team Main Street

The Real Estate Workshop teaches you how to build perpetual income for life, without going to work. Some of the topics include buying and selling paper, finding discounted properties, generating long-term monthly cash flow, and controlling properties wihtout owning them.

Real Estate Bootcamp
Presented by Wade B. Cook and Team Main Street

This three to four day Bootcamp is truly a roll-up-your-sleeves-and-do-the-deals event. You will be learning how to locate the bargains, negotiate strategies, and find wholesale properties (pre-foreclosures).

Business Entity Skills Training (BEST)
Presented by Wade B. Cook and Team Wall Street
Learn about the six powerful entities you can use to protect your wealth and your family. Learn the secrets of asset protection, eliminate your fear of litigation, and minimize your taxes.

Assorted Resources

Legal Forms
By Wade B. Cook
This collection of pertinent forms contains numerous legal forms used in real estate transactions. These forms were selected by experienced investors.

Record Keeping System
By Wade B. Cook
A complete record keeping system for organizing all of the information on each of your properties. This system keeps track of everything from insurance policies to equity growth.